BOBBY
FLAY

TOP CHEFS

OTHER TITLES IN THIS SERIES:

BOBBY FLAY

JOHN F. GRABOWSKI

Produced by OTTN Publishing, Stockton, New Jersey

Eldorado Ink
PO Box 100097
Pittsburgh, PA 15233
www.eldoradoink.com

CPSIA compliance information: Batch#TC010112-3. For further
information, contact Eldorado Ink at info@eldoradoink.com.

First printing

1 3 5 7 9 8 6 4 2

Library of Congress Cataloging-in-Publication Data

Grabowski, John F.
  Bobby Flay / John F. Grabowski.
      p. cm. — (Top chefs)
  Includes bibliographical references and index.
  ISBN 978-1-61900-010-0 (hc)
  ISBN 978-1-61900-011-7 (pb)
  ISBN 978-1-61900-012-4 (ebook)
  1. Flay, Bobby—Juvenile literature. 2. Cooks—New York (State)—New
York—Biography—Juvenile literature. 3. Celebrity chefs—New York
(State)—New York—Biography—Juvenile literature. I. Title.
  TX649.F54G73 2012
  641.5092—dc23
  [B]

                              2011044852

For information about custom editions, special sales, or
premiums, please contact our special sales department at
info@eldoradoink.com.

TABLE OF CONTENTS

Chef Bobby Flay works quickly to prepare a five-course meal on the popular television program Iron Chef America.

CHAPTER ONE

A KITCHEN BATTLE TO REMEMBER

C elebrity chefs have revolutionized the food industry and brought their profession into the public eye as never before. Superstar chefs reach millions of people through their restaurants, books, television shows, and commercial endorsements. In the process they have helped make people aware of the foods they consume. In a 2010 article, *Time* magazine reported, "[T]he phenomenon of the celebrity chef has utterly transformed the restaurant industry and, in the process, changed the very nature of how we eat."

One of the television shows responsible for this trend is *Iron Chef*, a popular Japanese program. And the person who helped spark interest in the show in the United States was a brash young American chef. His name is Bobby Flay.

IRON CHEF

Fuji TV produced *Ryori no Tetsujin*, or *Ironmen of Cooking*, which premiered on Japanese television in October 1993. The program was an innovative cooking competition hosted by the fictional character Takeshi Kaga. Known on the show as Chairman Kaga, the flashy host was famous for his outlandish, sequined formal men's attire, his fondness for biting into a crisp yellow pepper, and his cry of "Allez cuisine!" which is French for "Go cook!" or "Start cooking!" This command signaled the beginning of the competition. Kaga did not deny his eccentricities. He once said, "It's great to be known, but it's even better to be known as strange."

The basic storyline of the show was that Chairman Kaga was a wealthy, eccentric gourmet who invited famous chefs from around the world to competitions held in the grand "Kitchen Stadium" in his castle. The chefs would compete against the Chairman's Gourmet Academy, which was led by

CHAIRMAN TAKESHI KAGA

On *Iron Chef*, Chairman Kaga is a wealthy, eccentric gourmet who lives in a castle and stages competitions featuring his army of master chefs. In real life he is Shigekatsu Katsuda, a well-known star of Japanese stage and screen.

Born in 1950 in the Japanese city of Kanazawa, Katsuda was only seven years old when he joined the Kanazawa City Boys Choir. He soon moved on to an acting career. In 1972 he joined Gekidan Shiki, one of Japan's best-known theater companies, and had starring roles in such plays as *Jesus Christ Superstar*, *Les Misérables*, *Macbeth*, and *Jekyll and Hyde*. He also starred in several movies and hosted the Japanese game show *Time Shock 21*. Katsuda has been the voice of characters in animated films, including *Pokémon: Power of One* and *Black Jack: Two Doctors in Black*.

the Iron Chefs. These chefs specialized in Japanese, Chinese, French, and Italian cuisine.

The competition was a timed culinary battle. The chefs had 60 minutes to produce a full meal, consisting of three to five courses. Each course had to incorporate the show's theme ingredient—which was kept secret until filming. The secret ingredient ranged from the common, such as banana and asparagus, to the exotic, such as foie gras and truffles. Because of the show's Japanese origin, the secret ingredients were often foods common to Japan. They included tofu, river eel, and bamboo shoots. An announcer and commentator gave running accounts of the action as it occurred. At the end of the hour, a panel of judges tasted and rated the dishes to determined which chef was the winner.

The series was a gigantic hit in Japan. It ran for more than 300 episodes, before ending in 1999. That July, an English-dubbed version of the program started airing on U.S. television, on cable TV's Food Network. The program soon developed a cult following in the United States, with much of its allure coming from its dubbed voiceovers. It soon became one of the networks' most popular shows.

In 2000 Fuji TV produced two specials based on the original *Iron Chef* show. The first, broadcast in January on the Food Network, was called "The Millennium Special." It fea-

The secret ingredients on *Iron Chef* are not complete surprises to the competitors. They are given a list of five ingredients in advance, one of which will be the secret ingredient.

tured four chefs matching off in a pair of battles, with one of the winning dishes being named the Millennium Dish. The second special, "New York Battle," was broadcast two months later. It marked the first appearance of an American chef on the show.

"NEW YORK BATTLE"

The idea for "New York Battle" came from Tim and Nina Zagat, publishers of the popular restaurant guide *Zagat Survey*. The Zagats, who had served as judges on a previous *Iron Chef* show, invited four Japanese Iron Chefs to the United States with the intention of selecting one of them to compete against an American chef. The Iron Chef they ultimately selected was Masaharu Morimoto, head chef of the restaurant Nobu, located in New York City. He would compete against American chef Bobby Flay, the 36-year-old New York owner of Mesa Grill and Bolo in Manhattan. He was also host of the Food Network show *Hot Off the Grill with Bobby Flay*.

The battle took place in March 2000 in the landmark nightclub and concert site Webster Hall, in New York City. The site has played host to numerous rock stars, including Eric Clapton, Tina Turner, Prince, Aerosmith, B. B. King, and Guns N' Roses.

The Zagats served as two of the judges in the competition, which was filmed in front of a live audience. A third judge was actress and Food Network personality Donna Hanover, who was also the wife of New York City mayor Rudolph Giuliani. John Williams, a member of the studio audience, was selected at random to be a fourth judge.

At the beginning of the "New York Battle," Bobby Flay entered the hall making "raise the roof" movements with his hands. The audience immediately got into the act. People

Iron Chef Masaharu Morimoto was born in Hiroshima, Japan. He was employed as head chef of the prestigious Manhattan restaurant Nobu when he engaged in a memorable kitchen battle against Bobby Flay. Today, Morimoto operates restaurants in New York, Philadelphia, and Boca Raton, Florida.

Nina Zagat, who co-founded the Zagat Survey with her husband Tim in the early 1980s, has been called one of the most influential people in New York. She played a key role in introducing the Japanese cooking series Ryori no Tetsujin *to the United States, under the name* Iron Chef.

began whistling, cheering for their favorites, chanting the competitors' names, and holding up signs.

After the two chefs were introduced, the bottom half of a mirrored disco ball descended from the ceiling. Inside it was the theme ingredient for the battle: rock crab. Chairman Kaga signaled the start of the "New York Battle: Rock Crab," and the chefs and their assistants got to work.

The next hour proved torturous for Flay. He first had trouble using his food processor. And he received an electric shock from the range, which had faulty wiring. In an interview on the television series *Biography*, Flay explained, "I cut my finger, I almost cut my thumb off initially, and then I got electrically shocked by standing in water up to my ankles. And then the wires for the oven were running through it, and I was . . . getting thrown by the electricity."

At one point the sous chef asked if Flay wanted to quit because of the distractions and setbacks. Determined to see the competition through to the end, Bobby refused. Despite his problems in the kitchen, he managed to have his dishes prepared and plated by the time the closing bell signaled the end of the contest.

The Insult

After presenting his dishes, Flay climbed up onto the countertop of his kitchen area. He turned to the audience and in a moment of premature celebration pumped his arms in the air and shouted. Although these antics inspired his fans, other people were offended. They considered the behavior to be poor sportsmanship.

Flay's *Iron Chef* opponent was even more outspoken. When asked by the show's floor reporter for his views on the battle, Morimoto replied, "He's not a chef . . . after finishing, he stood up on the cutting board. That's not right. . . . Cutting boards and knives are sacred to us."

The Decision

After Morimoto made his comments, it was time for the judges' tasting. Morimoto's dishes were presented first. They included crab brain dip; crab rice in sour soup; crab hors d'oeuvres, two flavors; rock crabs grilled in seaweed; and Japanese crab salad. Bobby's creations came next. They consisted of crab and scallops in coriander sauce, rock crab salad, ethnic crab cakes, and spicy saffron soup. The scores were tabulated, and Chairman Kaga announced the results. The winner was Morimoto, by a score of 76 to 68.

In a 2008 *Forbes* magazine listing of the top-earning celebrity chefs, Rachael Ray topped the charts, with earnings of $18 million per year. Wolfgang Puck was second at $16 million, while Bobby Flay ranked ninth at $1.5 million.

Despite losing the contest, Flay believed his appearance on the show had a positive effect. After the Food Network broadcast "New York Battle" the following June, the media gave the controversy over the cutting board full coverage. In an interview with *Biography*, Bobby explained that the press said he disgraced the country and insulted Japan. All the publicity gave *Iron Chef* and the Food Network a boost. "It was the best thing that ever happened to the Food Network," Flay explained in an interview. "Because it brought them into what I consider pop culture. It went from some good cooking shows behind the stove to jotting down recipes to college campuses all around the country having Iron Chef competitions, I think, in one fell swoop."

The Food Network was not alone in benefiting from the popularity of the *Iron Chef* special. With his controversial appearance on the show, Flay found that his status as a celebrity chef and television entertainer was on the rise.

CHAPTER TWO

A KID WITHOUT DIRECTION

Bobby Flay is a native New Yorker, having been born and raised on the Upper East Side of Manhattan, one of the five boroughs of New York City. Bounded by 59th Street on the south, 96th Street on the north, Central Park on the west, and the East River on the east, the Upper East Side has been home to many of the city's wealthiest and most famous residents. These include first ladies Eleanor Roosevelt and Jacqueline Kennedy Onassis, film director Woody Allen, and the comedic family the Marx brothers.

The neighborhood's many attractions include the official residence of the New York City mayor, Gracie Mansion; the Metropolitan Museum of Art; the Solomon R. Guggenheim Museum; and the National Academy of Design. The area is also home to world-famous hotels such as the Plaza, Carlyle, and Pierre, and to fashionable Madison Avenue boutiques such as Louis Vuitton, Henri Bendel, and Monmartre.

THE LITTLEST CHEF

It was in this elegant residential neighborhood that Robert "Bobby" William Flay was born on December 10, 1964. He was the only child of William Flay, a Wall Street attorney, and Dorothy Flay, a paralegal for the cosmetic firm of Esteé Lauder.

A fourth-generation Irish-American, young Bobby had bright red hair, a multitude of freckles, and mischievous grin. Growing up, he was full of energy and very active. He enjoyed playing with his friends, and particularly liked sports. And at an early age, he demonstrated an interest in food.

Bobby was around five years old when he asked his mother for an Easy Bake oven for Christmas. The popular toy

Bobby Flay grew up in Manhattan's tony Upper East Side neighborhood.

used the heat generated by a light bulb to bake foods. "I just thought it was so cool that you could actually like bake a cake with a light bulb," he explained in a later interview. "It was at the top of his Christmas list," Dorothy told *People* magazine, "so I thought, 'why not?'" She gave her son the toy. But despite his early introduction to ovens, Bobby admits that baking is the weakest skill of his cooking repertoire.

Young Bobby soon graduated to more advanced kitchen projects. He made chocolate pudding, mixing the brown powder of packaged pudding mixes with milk to produce a creamy treat. He also helped his mother assemble deviled eggs and prepare other foods. He even gave her suggestions when she made up her shopping list for trips to the grocery store.

FAMILY COOKS

Bobby has said that his mother was a good, if not adventurous, cook. "My mom was an all-American cook in the 70's," he told a *New York Times* reporter. "She made pork chops and applesauce, lamb with mint jelly—no surprises. She wasn't sitting down with the *Gourmet* cookbook in her spare time."

Bobby has also spoken of fond memories of his grandmother's cooking. She often treated the family to her specialty—a marinated beef roast dish called sauerbraten. She would serve it with sweet-and-sour red cabbage, potatoes, and rye bread. The family would gather around the dinner table to enjoy the meal, although he recalled, his grandmother typically remained in the kitchen while the rest of the family ate.

Bobby's father also enjoyed cooking, and when he had the time, William Flay would try his hand at gourmet meals. During vacations at the New Jersey shore, Bobby's dad would host grilling parties, where he showcased his culinary skills. Bobby would help by cooking hamburgers, lobsters, and corn for family and friends who came to visit.

SPORTS AND FOOD

The Flays divorced when Bobby was around six years old. He lived with his mother in New York, but he remained close to his father. Bill Flay would eventually give up his law practice and embark on a new career. It was one that would have a considerable effect on young Bobby's future.

As Bobby grew older, he found that he had little interest in school. Doing homework and studying held little appeal. He preferred sports, and spent much of his time playing baseball and basketball with his friends. One summer, while away at camp, he was introduced to track and field. He developed a love of distance running that carried on through his high school years, and continues up to the present day.

When he was 12 years old, Bobby took his first job as a delivery boy at Mimi's Pizza, located on the Upper East Side. He also gained some experience in a restaurant kitchen. "I delivered pizzas in the sixth grade," he told the *New York Daily News*. "When I wasn't delivering pies, the owners of the parlor let me open the cans of tomatoes and grate the mozzarella." Three years later, Bobby graduated to scooping ice cream at the neighborhood Baskin-Robbins.

Bobby's tastes in food began to change. For example, as a teenager he came to prefer the hamburgers offered by the Upper East Side restaurants Jackson Hole Burgers and J. G. Melon. Rather than eat fast food hamburgers smothered in ketchup, onions, and American cheese, he preferred burgers adorned with toppings like bacon, mushrooms, chili, guacamole, peppers, barbeque sauce, and a wide variety of cheeses.

However, Bobby's attitude toward school did not change. He made no plans for the future, other than meeting his friends for a game of basketball or baseball. But his dreams of finding glory and fame in the sports world eventually came crashing down. He would later tell an interviewer that when growing up he knew what he wanted to be: "A professional athlete. Either a basketball or baseball player, until I got to high school and realized it was never going to happen."

Not Made for School

While in high school, Bobby lost interest in cooking. He was bored in class and not interested in anything that was not related to sports. He became more rebellious and impulsive, taking more chances and breaking rules. In the morning he and his friends would meet at the subway station at 77th Street and Lexington Avenue with the intention of heading off to high school. But if the subway car was full, they would skip school. "We used to have this rule," he told *ABC News Nightline*, "my friends and I . . . if it was too crowded to get on the first subway, we went to breakfast. And maybe that was the beginning of my food career, a Greek diner in New York."

Bobby has joked that he attended every Catholic school in the city, including Xavier High School, from which he was asked to leave not once, but twice. Book learning was not his strong suit. His classroom was the street. In an interview with Food Network's *Chefography*, he explained, "People [who] don't know my school history will say to me, 'Where did you go to college?' And I say to them, 'Well, I went to UCLA.' And they say, 'You did? In California?' And I'm like, 'No, University of the Corner of Lexington Avenue.'"

Bobby's main extracurricular activity became hanging out on street corners with his friends. Although they didn't con-

Although Bobby Flay did not graduate from Xavier High School in Manhattan, several other notables did, including television personality Al Roker, U.S. Supreme Court justice Antonin Scalia, and former New York City mayor Jimmy Walker.

sider themselves a gang, it still was a pretty tough group of kids. His lack of interest, poor grades, and poor attendance eventually led him to drop out of high school at age 17. It did not take long for his father to decide a change was in order.

JOE ALLEN RESTAURANT

After Bill Flay gave up his Wall Street law practice, he met a man named Joe Allen. Allen owned Joe Allen Restaurant on West 46th Street, in Manhattan's theater district. Since its opening in 1965, the restaurant had established a policy to serve good food at reasonable prices. Its regular clientele included numerous theatrical and show business personalities, including comedian Rosie O'Donnell and actor Al Pacino.

Bill Flay became the restaurant's manager and eventually a partner in the business with Joe. Bobby once explained how his father came to be hired:

> My sense was Joe thought to himself, 'Well, you know, eventually this could be a good situation because I could have somebody who really understands business, who's an attorney, who could help grow this business.'. . . My father didn't know the restaurant business at all. So basically what he did was, he said, 'Look, give me $200 a week. I want to learn the business, I want to work behind the bar, and I want to work on the door, I want to wait tables, I want to know everybody's job because if I'm gonna be the boss, I need to know exactly what they need to do.'

Realizing that college was not an option for Bobby, Bill Flay sat his son down for a talk. He told Bobby if he wasn't going to go to school, he had to get a job. Knowing his father was serious, the boy agreed. The next day he received a call from his father, informing Bobby that he had a job at the restaurant.

Years later, Bobby would recall his father's words: "The busboy had to leave to take care of his grandmother. You're going to fill in. . . . And don't forget: no special treatment. Because you're my son, you better work harder than anyone else. Put your head down, do your job and don't aggravate anybody—including me."

In addition to his original restaurant in New York's theater district, Joe Allen has opened Joe Allen restaurants in London and Paris.

DEVELOPING AN INTEREST

It was 1981 when Bobby began working at Joe Allen. He cleared and set tables and performed other menial tasks, but without much enthusiasm. He got up in the morning, did his job, and came back home at night.

The busboy returned two weeks later, and Bobby was walking out the door when the chef called after him and asked if he wanted a job in the kitchen. Bobby accepted the offer. He later admitted he agreed to take the job simply because he had nothing better to do.

The duties for the entry-level job included stocking the pantry and washing dishes. But the chef soon had Bobby chopping vegetables and making salads. To his surprise, he found that he enjoyed working with food. He later wrote,

> I remember waking up one morning, staring at the ceiling and saying to myself, I'm really looking forward to going to work today. . . . From that point forward, I looked at work differently. I enjoyed it. I felt I was contributing. Slowly, I was shedding my irresponsible 17-year-old skin.

Bobby became motivated to learn more about the art of cooking. At home, he read cookbooks and articles in food magazines in order to keep up with new developments and trends in the industry. He watched cooking shows on television. One of his favorite cooking personalities was Julia Child, who had gained fame in the 1960s as author of the cookbook *Mastering the Art of French Cooking* and host of *The French Chef* on television. Another favorite chef was Graham Kerr, who hosted a popular television program called *The Galloping Gourmet.*

BACK TO SCHOOL

But Bobby had a great deal to learn about cooking. And after a while, Joe Allen recognized that the young man had potential. When he first hired Bobby, Allen had had serious doubts. He was a high school dropout with a know-it-all, wise guy attitude. Joe would later say that at first he hadn't thought that Bobby was cut out for a future in the restaurant business.

WOLFGANG PUCK

The rise of the celebrity chef in the United States dates to the early 1980s when Austrian-born master chef Wolfgang Puck opened Spago restaurant in Los Angeles, California. Flay credits Puck for introducing the American people to great, whimsical, non-French food and, by extension, to his own cuisine.

Puck came to the United States in 1973 at the age of 25. Nine years later, in 1982, he opened Spago on the Sunset Strip in West Hollywood. The restaurant featured dishes pioneered by Puck that came to be known as "California cuisine." His designer pizzas and pastas attracted actors, actresses, producers, and politicians. Spago soon became one of the most famous restaurants in the country.

In 1997 Puck opened Spago Beverly Hills and renamed the original eatery Spago Hollywood. The new restaurant eventually surpassed the original in popularity, and Spago Hollywood closed its doors in March 2001.

But Allen saw Bobby's efforts in the kitchen and soon changed his mind. One day he called the teen into the office and told him about a new cooking school that was opening in New York. Founded by Dorothy Cann, the school was called the French Culinary Institute (FCI). Joe thought it would be the perfect place for Bobby to learn classical French cuisine.

At first Bobby hesitated. He didn't want to return to the classroom, but Joe soon convinced him that he would not be spending all his time sitting in class listening to lectures. He would also be getting valuable hands-on experience in the kitchen as he learned how to prepare and plate dishes. Reading, writing, and arithmetic would be replaced by sautéing, flambéing, and braising. Despite his aversion to school, Bobby finally agreed to go.

Before he could enroll at the school, however, Bobby needed to take—and pass—a high school equivalency exam. He succeeded and went on to join FCI's first class of 11 students when the institute opened its doors in March 1984. At the age of 19, he was the youngest student.

On the first day of classes, Bobby received an unexpected gift. Joe Allen handed him a check. He was paying the full tuition. There were no conditions attached to this gift. Joe did not expect Bobby to repay him in any way, other than by doing his best. It was an act of generosity Bobby would never forget.

CHAPTER THREE

EDUCATION OF A CHEF

Bobby Flay was in the first class accepted into the French Culinary Institute, a new school in New York City that had been inspired by its founder's love of French cuisine. In the 1960s and 1970s, Brooklyn-born Dorothy Cann had attended college in England and traveled to France during her vacation time. After spending three years in Thailand as a volunteer with the Peace Corps, she returned to the United States in 1974.

Cann took a job working as a receptionist for her father, who owned Apex Technical School, in Brooklyn. In 1978, after working her way up through the ranks, she became director of the trade school. In the early 1980s she was invited to visit some of the top trade schools in France. One of them was Ecoles Grégoire Ferrandi in Paris, a well-known training ground for new chefs.

FRENCH CULINARY INSTITUTE

When Dorothy returned home she talked to her father about having Apex start a school in New York City to train chefs. She

Dorothy Cann Hamilton founded the French Culinary Institute, where Bobby Flay received formal training as a chef. He was a member of the institute's first graduating class in 1984.

told an interviewer, "I convinced my father that we should open a cooking school and use the French school—not only as a model—but we actually paid the French government for the curriculum, they brought over the teachers and they maintained the quality control." The result was the French Culinary Institute (FCI).

For the first two years, the school was run as a joint program with the Ferrandi School. Later, it established a program using chefs based in the United States.

The FCI curriculum centers on the 250 classic culinary techniques that are the basis of traditional French cuisine. Courses of study include career programs in classic culinary arts, classic pastry arts, and the art of international bread baking. Specialized training is also available in courses such as the fundamentals of wine, cake techniques and design, the science of food and cooking, and restaurant management.

HANDS-ON EXPERIENCE

As the French Culinary Institute was starting up in March 1984, it experienced some problems. During the first week of classes, Con Edison, the giant utility company that provides gas and electricity to much of New York City, turned off the school's gas supply. There was no fuel for the stoves and ovens, so classes had to be cancelled and the school's instructor and 11 students were sent home.

Early in the same week Cann received an unexpected phone call from Sara Moulton, who was chef at the executive dining room at *Gourmet* magazine. Cookbook author and television personality Julia Child wanted to come for a meal that Friday and to see the school. Dorothy's initial thought, she later told an interviewer, was that the idea "was ridiculous, because I didn't have any students."

Preparing a meal on such short notice and without working gas ranges proved a challenge. But the school's first instructor, chef Antoine Shaeffers, made do with portable propane burners. The lunch prepared for Child was a success. The meal so impressed her that she featured the school on a segment of the news and talk show *Good Morning America*.

Despite his initial reluctance to return to school, Bobby quickly came to enjoy his experiences at the French Culinary Institute. The school opened up a whole new world to him— the world of classical French cooking. Bobby would later say that the FCI gave him a foundation, and provided him with the basics that he continues to use today.

In August 1984 Flay completed the intensive six-month course of study and graduated from the culinary school. He went back to work at Joe Allen, with the thought that his career path would eventually lead to more responsibilities at the restaurant or in helping Joe open another eatery. His benefactor, however, had different plans for him. A few months after graduation, Joe gently pushed Bobby out the door. There was nothing more for him to learn at Joe Allen Restaurant. It was time for Bobby to move on and expand his horizons.

MOVING ON UP

Flay did not stay unemployed for long. His diploma from the French Culinary Institute helped him land a job in 1985 as a sous chef at the Brighton Grill, a new restaurant on the Upper East Side. He was only on the job for just two days when one of the owners informed him that he was being promoted. The owner told him the head chef had drunk so much tequila the night before that he passed out in the restaurant. "He's fired," the owner said. "You're the chef now."

Bobby spent the next year at the Brighton Grill, where he continued to learn his craft, perfect his techniques, and apply his newly learned skills. But he realized he was not yet ready to run a kitchen on his own. He felt overwhelmed trying to do all the jobs it involved. "I was 20 years old, and way over my head," he told the *Wall Street Journal*. "I had to hire the cooks and do the menus. I did it for a year, but I thought, I need to know how to cook better."

CALIFORNIA CUISINE

After meeting chef Jonathan Waxman, Bobby put his thoughts into action. Waxman was an important figure on the New York culinary scene. In 1984 the renowned chef had opened Jams on Manhattan's East 79th Street. A short time later, he opened a second restaurant, called Bud's, on the Upper West Side. Both restaurants featured California and

Jonathan Waxman once earned a scholarship to the University of Nevada for playing the trombone. He later performed with a rock group called Lynx.

New York chef Jonathan Waxman became known for bringing the new "California cuisine" concept pioneered by Wolfgang Puck to the East Coast in the early 1980s. He would prove to be a mentor to Bobby Flay.

Southwestern cuisine, which was a novelty on the East Coast.

California cuisine makes use of fresh meats, fruits, and vegetables, many of which are organic. This means they are produced without the use of chemical fertilizers or insecticides. The animals are raised without being given antibiotics or growth hormones. Andre Sfez, owner of the California-style restaurant Batons in Greenwich Village, described the food for *Nation's Restaurant News*: "California cuisine is the best of what people today are cooking. The food is great; it's what you call healthy. All those grills and vegetables."

In the mid-1980s chefs were starting to create excitement about food, and Waxman was one of the best known. Both of his restaurants, Jams and Bud's, were earning glowing reviews as the new cuisine caught on. At the time Flay met Waxman, the celebrity chef was a darling of the media, renowned for helping elevate American cuisine in the culinary world. Michael Batterberry, editor and publisher of *Food Arts* magazine, told the *New York Times*, "Whoever said chefs of the 80's were like rock-and-roll stars had Jonathan in mind."

UNDER WAXMAN'S WING

Bobby soon had the opportunity to join one of Waxman's restaurants. He attended a cocktail party at the French Culinary Institute, where he met Gail Arnold, the chef at Bud's. Within five minutes of meeting her, he was offered a job as a line cook. A line cook, also known as a station chef or chef de partie, is in charge of a particular area or department in the kitchen.

Bobby accepted the job immediately. He would later say that the time he spent as a line cook at Bud's was one of the most enjoyable periods of his culinary career. "I loved the

THE SCOVILLE SCALE

In 1912 Wilbur Scoville, an American pharmacologist with the drug company Parke-Davis, developed a method to measure the amount of heat in a chili pepper. Known as the Scoville Organoleptic Test, it measures the amount of capsaicin in the pepper. Capsaicin is the chemical substance responsible for the heat. The compound is produced at the point where the ribs of the pepper meet the pod wall and is concentrated in the ribs.

The Scoville scale ranges from a value of 0 units for sweet bell peppers, which have no capsaicin at all, to 350,000 units for Mexican habaneros. Values vary, however, since the scale is based on human subjectivity and is not precise.

A newer test using a machine called a high-pressure liquid chromatograph provides a more accurate measurement of the amount of capsaicin in peppers. The unit of measure is still called the Scoville in the pharmacologist's honor.

camaraderie of it," he told an interviewer. "I loved the energy of it. I loved being in the heat of being busy. I felt like I was part of a team." The time spent working for Waxman would prove to be a turning point in his career.

The cooks at Bud's, including Waxman, introduced Flay to a range of vibrant flavors with which he had been completely unfamiliar. He explained, "They introduced me to blue corn tortillas, poblano peppers, ancho chiles, mangoes, papayas, black beans, tomatillos, and cilantro. They showed me that there could be real excitement and pride in American food."

For Bobby, it was love at first bite. The tastes, textures, aromas, heat, and pungency of Southwestern food enchanted him. He looked forward to coming to work each day, learning as much as he could by picking the brains of everyone at the restaurant. Waxman became his culinary guru. Bobby credits him with being the first person to teach him about good food.

In May 1986 Waxman opened a French bistro on the Upper East Side called Hulot's. Bobby went to work at the restaurant, under chef Stephanie Lyness and sous chef Paul Del Favero. "It was closed on Sundays," he explained. "But here's how passionate I'd become about cooking: Another chef and I would get the keys from the manager and show up there on Sunday afternoons—when the place was closed— just to cook. For fun. That's when I knew cooking was my life." At Hulot's, Paul Del Favero helped Flay hone his basic French culinary skills.

A SIGNATURE STYLE

Inspired by Waxman—and with his mentor's blessing— Bobby looked to further his culinary education. He took some time off to travel around the country. He concentrated on Texas, Arizona, and New Mexico, where he could learn more about Southwestern cuisine. He worked in kitchens throughout that part of the country, trying to absorb everything he could learn about the regional dishes.

One of the things that Bobby discovered about his profession was a willingness among chefs to share ideas, tips, and recipes with one another. In his travels he worked with well-known chefs such as Robert Del Grande of Cafe Annie in Houston, Stephen Pyles in Dallas, Dean Fearing of Fearing's at the Ritz-Carlton in Dallas, Kevin Rathbun in Atlanta, and Mark Kiffin of The Compound Restaurant in Santa Fe, New Mexico. He became acquainted with foods, ingredients and flavors foreign to the average New York chef. And he found that although the competition between chefs can be fierce, the friendship and camaraderie is even stronger. "I was a New York City kid wanting to do their food," he told the *New York Times*, "and they were incredibly generous with their time and knowledge."

Flay gradually began to develop his own style. His approach in creating dishes was to combine the flavors of the American Southwest with those of Mediterranean cuisine. Bobby continued to work at his craft every day, trying out new recipes and re-inventing old ones.

After Flay returned to New York, he attempted a "career experiment." He left Waxman and briefly worked as a stockbroker's assistant on the floor of the American Stock Exchange. But that situation did not last long.

After a few unfulfilling months, Bobby returned to cooking. At the age of 23 he secured a job as head chef at the Miracle Grill, a new Southwestern restaurant owned by Lynn Loflin and Rich Kresberg. Opened in 1988 in East

The cooking style known as "Southwestern cuisine" blends influences from Native Americans, Mexicans, Spanish colonists, and 19th-century American cowboys, and ranchers. Southwestern cuisine can vary greatly from state to state; however, recipes typically incorporate a variety of chilies, spices, beans, and fresh ingredients common to the region.

Greenwich Village, the eatery was one of the first in New York City to feature Southwestern cuisine. Within a few months Flay made the Miracle Grill into one of the city's hottest new restaurants.

COOKING WITH REGIS PHILBIN

Flay soon caught the attention of the media, and he was invited to make his first appearance on television. It was a spot on the popular *Regis and Kathie Lee* morning show starring Regis Philbin and Kathie Lee Gifford. The young chef found that performing on the small screen was more difficult than he thought it would be. "I remember having very little energy because I was so nervous," Bobby told *TV Guide*. He described making several mistakes:

> I didn't smile. I think I had to make a potato salad because it was summer, and I just remember thinking how good Regis was because he kept the segment going. You just have to continue to do it and make the mistakes just so you can get better at it over time. It takes awhile. . . . The hardest thing to do is be yourself on television.

As the future would show, the young chef was a quick learner. In time Bobby would become a fixture on the small screen.

MARRIAGE

In June 1990 Flay was cooking at a benefit for Meals-on-Wheels, a charity organization that provides meals to homebound needy senior citizens, when he met another participating chef named Debra Ponzek. She was the chef at Montrachet, a well-known French restaurant located in the area of south Manhattan known as TriBeCa (the Triangle Below Canal Street).

A 1984 graduate from the Culinary Institute of America, Debra Ponzek was named in 1989 as one of the "Ten Best New American Chefs" by *Food and Wine*. In 1990, the Chefs of America Association honored her as "Chef of the Year."

In hopes of making a good impression on her, Bobby invited Debra and five of her friends to dinner at the Miracle Grill, where he cooked them an elegant meal. It included mussel and cilantro soup, black bean cakes, and shrimp and roasted garlic tamales.

The two chefs began seeing each other regularly and within a few weeks Bobby proposed. Debra accepted, and they were married the following May. In a *New York Times* article covering the upcoming wedding, Bobby explained his admiration for Ponzek, who was a prominent New York chef. "I have a great deal of respect for her," he said. "Women in this profession don't get a lot of good shakes." However, the marriage would not last long. Bobby and Debra would divorce two years later.

Bobby visits a fruit market in Manhattan. During the early 1990s, he opened two very successful restaurants in New York City: Mesa Grill and Bolo.

CHAPTER FOUR

FINDING NEW FLAVORS

As chef at Miracle Grill, Flay continued to receive praise for his innovative cuisine. His inventive use of Southwestern ingredients made the restaurant a success in New York's very competitive restaurant scene. That experience gave him the confidence to follow his dream.

Ever since he decided that cooking was what he wanted to do with his life, Bobby wanted his own restaurant. His ideas about this restaurant were very specific, and he described them in the introduction to one of his cookbooks:

> I imagined soaring ceilings, dramatic colors adorning the walls, a large bar on one side of the room but not separate from the dining room. I wanted a sense of energy. I wanted a restaurant that would take you to another place as soon as you walked in the front door. An experience that was unique unto itself. And, of course, my dream restaurant would be in New York City, my birthplace.

Opening a restaurant is an expensive and risky business. A recent study by researchers at Ohio State University found that up to 60 percent of restaurants fail within three years. In major cities like New York, the failure rate is even higher.

In 1990 Flay decided it was time for him to turn his dream into a reality. He was ready to open a restaurant of his own.

A NEW PARTNERSHIP

Owning and operating a restaurant involves a lot more than just cooking food, so Bobby turned to his father for advice. After all, Bill Flay had a great deal of experience from managing Joe Allen Restaurant. Bobby and his father considered going into a venture together, but while they were still in the process of scouting out possible locations for their future business, another opportunity arose.

Jerome Kretchmer, the owner of one of New York City's culinary landmarks, the Gotham Bar and Grill, came to Miracle Grill with his wife. Jerome and Dorothy Kretchmer had just returned from a trip to the American Southwest, and the prominent restaurateur was thinking about opening a restaurant specializing in the cuisine of that region.

Jerome asked Bobby if he would be interested in joining him in the venture. Flay considered the offer attractive, but he hesitated to accept since he had already discussed a business partnership with his father. He later wrote how he was relieved when his father advised, "Do it with him. That way you and I can just be father and son."

MESA GRILL

Kretchmer and Flay found a site for the new restaurant on Fifth Avenue, between 15th Street and 16th Streets. Kretchmer and another partner, Jeff Bliss, would take charge of the financial arrangements for the new venture, while Flay would serve as executive chef.

Kretchmer had definite plans for the restaurant. In an interview aired on *Biography*, Flay explained:

> Jerry said, 'Let's wake this place up. Let's open this restaurant for New York. Let's have some fun. . . . Let's open a restaurant with a value-driven menu and a lot of energy and a lot of color.' And that's what Mesa Grill opened as. It was this big, sort of loud— both in sound and in color and in flavor—restaurant.

Mesa Grill opened its doors on January 15, 1991, but the restaurant's first day did not go as well as expected. It was the same week that President George H. W. Bush announced the beginning of an air war against Iraq. Flay explained:

> Although New York was in a deadly financial recession, opening night of Mesa Grill was raucous . . . until the first bomb was dropped on Iraq, signaling the start of the First Gulf War. Half of the dining room got up from their tables to go home and watch the first-ever televised war. It was not an illustrious start.

It did not take long, however, for the restaurant to earn positive reviews. Critics from the *New York Times* and the *Village Voice* raved about the exciting new flavors and dishes being prepared by executive chef Bobby Flay. *Times* restaurant critic Bryan Miller wrote that "the sassy Tex-Mex fare at Mesa Grill surpasses anything of its kind elsewhere in New

York City." A year later Gael Greene, the respected food critic for *New York Magazine*, bestowed on the eatery the title "Best Restaurant of 1992."

The contemporary Southwestern cuisine that everyone raved about featured a blend of flavors and ingredients that were new to many New Yorkers. Bobby described the Southwestern foods found at his restaurant:

> The roasted corn fresh from the cob; the cornmeals in a myriad of colors; the dried red chiles that are earthy, smoky, fruity, and spicy; the fresh chiles that are peppery, herbaceous, and mouthwatering; the ripe, creamy avocados; the sweet fruits like mango and papaya; pineapples hot off the grill, ready to be made into a salsa; the meats, fish and vegetables that are gently rubbed with spices to accent their flavors and help create a crust that is savory and mouth tingling; the glazes and barbecue sauces; the marinades and rubs; and don't forget the tequila.

The Kretchmer and Flay collaboration was a rousing success. Kretchmer later told *People* magazine, "My first take on Bobby was that he was really intelligent, a little bit tough and very cute, and therefore incredibly marketable. Then I realized he can really cook too."

Part of Bobby's success came from his ability to borrow ideas from other chefs and incorporate them into his own cuisine. Taking another person's ideas is a common practice among chefs. Jonathan Waxman, for example, admits to having pilfered some of chef Mark Miller's ideas and creations. Flay, in turn, admits to appropriating Waxman's cuisine. The end result of this synthesis was a cooking style that made Bobby one of the hottest chefs in New York City.

ANOTHER VENTURE

Determined to continue expanding his culinary horizons, Flay traveled to Spain, where he encountered the rustic, full-flavored ingredients and foods of Madrid, Barcelona, and other cities of the country. His love of Spanish cuisine and the success of Mesa Grill eventually inspired Bobby to start planning another eatery—one with a Mediterranean-style cuisine.

This time Flay partnered with Jerome Kretchmer's son Laurence. Together, they spent a year and a half searching for the right location for their business. Laurence explained to *Nation's Restaurant News* why it took so long to settle on a site: "We looked at 50 to 100 different restaurants, but there

GAEL GREENE, FOOD CRITIC

One of the most famous restaurant critics in the United States is Gael Greene, whose regular column appeared in *New York* magazine for more than 30 years. She is also a successful author, who has produced both fiction and non-fiction books.

Greene's most important contribution to the food world, however, does not involve writing. In 1981 she cofounded Citymeals-on-Wheels. The organization was formed to provide nutritious food to homebound and elderly New Yorkers. Today, the organization supplies approximately 2 million meals each year to over 16,000 New Yorkers. Her work earned her the James Beard Foundation's 1992 Humanitarian of the Year Award.

Bobby Flay poses with his girlfriend, actress Stephanie March (center), and Laurence Kretchmer (left), his partner in the New York restaurant Bolo.

was always a problem: either the landlord was stubborn, or they didn't have the right equipment."

The two partners finally chose the site of a former restaurant on East 22nd Street. Much of the equipment from the previous occupant was still in place, so it cost just $250,000 to get the eatery ready for business. In comparison, it had cost $300,000 to open Mesa Grill two years earlier. At the time, spending $1 million and up to outfit a restaurant was not unheard of in New York City.

BOLO

Flay and Kretchmer named the new venture after themselves, "Bo" for Bobby and "Lo" for Laurence. The new Spanish-themed restaurant, named Bolo, opened its doors in November 1993. It was time for New York to acknowledge the flavor and cuisine of Spain, Bobby told an interviewer. "Spain is the forgotten culinary country," he explained. "There's only a couple of Spanish restaurants here, and you either have old places with cheap wine or traditional places like Paradis Barcelona. We're not into educating; we just want to challenge customers' palates a bit."

Flay combined American ingredients with Mediterranean-style cooking, creating recipes for Bolo that featured his unique style but retained their distinct Spanish flavors. However, one thing was missing from the menu—the Spanish appetizers known as tapas. In Spain, tapas are often served at bars where patrons go before eating their midday or evening meal. They are finger foods, served warm or cold, that are usually offered to allow a diner to sample various foods without filling up before the main course. Occasionally, they are eaten as a meal in themselves.

When he opened Bolo, Flay was reluctant to put tapas on the menu. He didn't think restaurant customers would want to stand at a bar juggling little plates of food while trying to enjoy their drink.

AWARDS AND HONORS

The new restaurant's lack of tapas did not cause problems. Numerous positive reviews from food critics helped cement Bobby's reputation as one of the leading chefs in New York City. That reputation was enhanced by a pair of awards he won the same year that Bolo opened. One was the Outstanding Graduate Award from the French Culinary Institute. The other was an award from the prestigious James Beard Foundation.

The Foundation was established in 1986 in honor of James Beard, a renowned chef who in the 1940s hosted the first cooking TV show, and who published many cookbooks. In 1954 the *New York Times* called Beard the dean of American cookery. The following year, he established the James Beard Cooking School.

The year after the chef's death in 1985, the James Beard Foundation was established in New York City. Its mission, according to its website, is "To celebrate, nurture, and preserve America's diverse culinary heritage and future." In 1990 the organization began presenting the James Beard Foundation Awards, often referred to as the Oscars of the food world. The awards pay tribute to the country's finest chefs, restaurants, cookbook authors, and other culinary professionals.

Bobby received the James Beard Foundation Rising Star Chef Award in 1993. The award goes to the country's most accomplished chef under the age of 30.

A CHANGING MENU

Tapas eventually did make their way onto the menu at Bolo. During one of their trips to Spain, Bobby and Stephanie March—his girlfriend at the time—sampled them often. When Stephanie suggested that he introduce them to Bolo, Bobby agreed.

Flay created a new tapas menu for the restaurant that debuted in 2003. It was greeted with positive reviews. A reviewer with the *New York Times* wrote, "The new tapas menu shows Mr. Flay at his best. It forces him to work in miniature, a format that shows off his talent for expressing simple flavors clearly, with precise seasoning. . . . Bolo has rediscovered its youth, and, improbably become fresher and more vibrant than the day it opened." The *New York Times* awarded Bolo two stars while the *Zagat's Survey* rated it the top Spanish restaurant in New York City.

Although Bobby earned raves for his Spanish cuisine at Bolo, he has had some dishes at Bolo that failed miserably. When asked by a viewer of *Late Night with Jimmy Fallon* about his worst cooking disaster, he mentioned an ill-fated lobster and duck paella dish he created in 1984. "All my friends told me it was terrible," he said, "including my staff at my restaurant. I was like, 'You guys don't know what you're talking about.' But then finally the *New York Times* restaurant critic came in and just crushed the dish."

But for the most part, Bolo continued to earn rave reviews during its stay on the New York restaurant scene. It served customers for 14 years, and did not close its doors until December 31, 2007. The building in which it was located had been sold for $12.5 million, and was slated to be demolished and replaced by a luxury condominium tower.

FLEDGLING AUTHOR

During the 1990s Mesa Grill was one of the most talked-about restaurants in New York. People were constantly asking Bobby for the recipes for some of his dishes. So he decided to provide that information in a cookbook.

Bobby Flay's Bold American Food hit the bookstores in May 1994. The graphically stunning volume contained many of his favorite recipes from Mesa Grill. And like the restaurant, the book was a smash hit. It also won the 1995 International Association of Culinary Professionals award for design.

In 1995 Flay was a successful restaurant owner and cookbook author. And soon another opportunity would come his way—one that would bring him recognition not only in New York, but around the entire country.

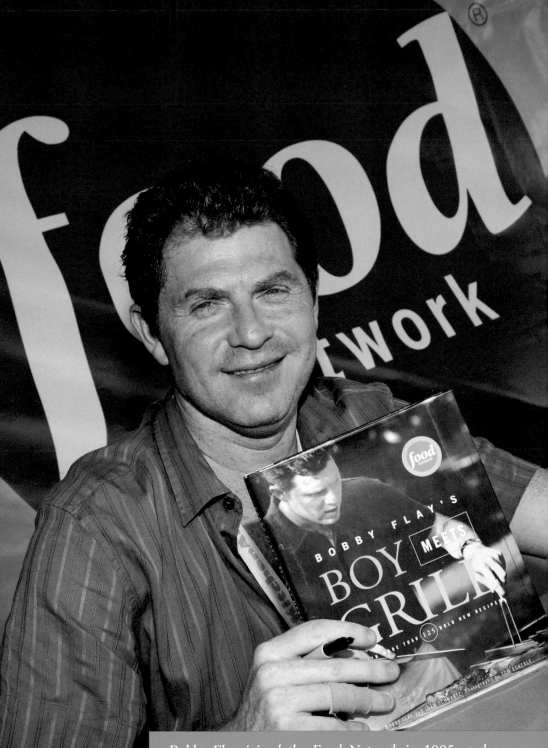

Bobby Flay joined the Food Network in 1995, and soon became one of its biggest stars. His Food Network programs made Bobby a national celebrity and helped him promote his restaurants and cookbooks.

CHAPTER FIVE

THE FOOD NETWORK

In the late 1970s cable television networks began narrowcasting, or catering to specific audience interest groups. For example, the Entertainment Sports Programming Network (ESPN) launched in 1979 to give sports fans 24-hour-a-day access to games and sports-driven shows. Two years later Music Television (MTV) began broadcasting music videos. During the 1990s another network would narrowcast television programs on the subject of cooking and food.

THE TV FOOD NETWORK

On November 23, 1993, the TV Food Network (TVFN) debuted on cable television. It would later be known as the Food Network. The network was the brainchild of Maurice "Reese" Schonfeld, an American television journalist who in the early 1980s was the founding president of Cable News Network (CNN). In 1993 he developed TVFN in conjunction with the Providence Journal Company.

The TV Food Network began broadcasting with a lineup that included chefs Curtis Aikens, Emeril Lagasse, Jacques

Pépin, and David Rosengarten; eating specialist Dr. Louis Arrone; cookbook author and company CEO Debbi Fields; and news journalists Donna Hanover and Robin Leach. The network received a big boost when it purchased the rights to broadcast reruns of the classic Julia Child series *The French Chef*. Other programs starring chefs Mario Batali, Mary Sue Milliken, Susan Feniger, and Michelle Urvater added to the network's growing popularity.

KATE CONNELLY

In January 1995 Bobby was a guest on the Food Network show *Robin Leach Talking Food*. Cohosting the show was Kate Connelly, a 31-year-old divorcee. After the show, Bobby invited Kate out for dinner. Kate later said it was the most enjoyable date of her life.

Soon Bobby and Kate were seeing each other regularly. He proposed a couple months later and she accepted. They were married the following October at Bolo Restaurant. Flay was not only becoming a husband again, but also a stepfather—Kate had an eight year old son from a previous marriage. In an interview with the *New York Times*, he acknowledged that married life might not be easy. "It's a complicated situation and the odds are against us," he said, "but that's what's great about it. If there's no challenge, why do it?"

In April 1996 Kate gave birth to a daughter, Sophie. But unfortunately, Bobby's words proved to be prophetic. The marriage faced problems that could not be worked out, and the couple soon divorced.

TELEVISION PERSONALITY

Meanwhile, Flay was finding time to share his enthusiasm for food before television audiences. In the mid-1990s he

A number of the Food Network's most popular chefs are pictured at an awards ceremony. The man holding the microphone near the center of the photo is Emeril Lagasse, a renowned New Orleans chef who has been one of the Food Network's biggest stars since it began broadcasting in the early 1990s.

appeared in several episodes of the Discovery Channel series *Great Chefs*. The show featured chefs cooking favorite dishes from their restaurants. In 1996 Bobby hosted *The Main Ingredient* on the Lifetime network. He realized the exposure was great publicity for his restaurants.

Bobby also spent a week cooking on a Food Network show called *Chef du Jour*. Each week a different chef led viewers through the preparation of gourmet meals. In a way, chefs participating on the program were auditioning for future projects on the Food Network. Although Bobby later said that he did not think he did particularly well when he appeared on the program, Food Network producers saw his potential. In 1996 he was invited to join the cable channel's regular lineup.

The opportunity to appear on the cable television show came about in part because Bobby lived and worked in New York City, which was also the location of the Food Network studios. He would later say, only half kidding, that because of a lack of funds, the network signed only local chefs who could get to the studios by taxi or subway. In an interview with the PBS television series *Chef's Story*, he explained:

> The Food Network opened in New York and they [had] zero dollars. . . . New cable network, they're in some shabby studio on the West Side. . . . Then they started to grow and become more successful and they actually offered me a show. . . . They wanted a grilling show and they said . . . 'You know that guy Jack McDavid [owner of Jack's Firehouse in Philadelphia] that's a friend of yours? . . . Can you call him and ask him if he'd like to do a show with you?. . . That was, really, the way it happened. And Jack and I went to Clearwater, Florida, and we shot forty-two half-hour shows in six days . . . seven a day.

The outdoor barbecuing series was called *Grillin' and Chillin'*. It featured Bobby as the city boy who grilled with gas, and Jack as the country boy who believed in slow grilling with charcoal. The good-natured competition between the two accounted for a significant part of the show's appeal.

BOBBY AND JACQUI

The success of Bobby's first show for the Food Network led to a second one, *Hot Off the Grill with Bobby Flay*, which debuted in 1998. Although Bobby's name was the only one in the show's title, Flay worked with a cohost—actress and stand-up comedian Jacqui Malouf. Jacqui was a Food

Network regular who had hosted *Sara Moulton's Cooking Live*, *Superbowl Food*, and *Cruising the Caribbean*. She had also appeared on *Seasons Eatings* and *Viva Lagasse*. The friendly banter between Bobby and Jacqui added to the program's popularity.

Hot Off the Grill with Bobby Flay firmly established Bobby's reputation as a master griller. He has said that he finds it ironic that he became famous for grilling in a studio (the show was filmed in a SoHo loft) rather than outdoors, which was the setting for *Grillin' and Chillin'*. The show lasted for more than 300 episodes before ending its run.

FOODNATION

Meanwhile, Flay had signed on to do another show. This one was unlike the previous two in one important way: it didn't require that he do any cooking. *FoodNation with Bobby Flay* followed the chef as he traveled around the country and sampled the food of various regions. The program, which first aired in June 2000, featured interviews with local cooks and discussions of each area's culinary history and character. Flay would later write:

> [B]y traveling around the country I [was] privileged to meet so many wonderful people who were cooking, smoking, deep-frying, steaming, and baking these amazing regional dishes. Filming the show across America . . . really opened my eyes to how incredibly rich our country is when it comes to our food and the people who cook it.

Around the same time that the first episode of *FoodNation* aired, Flay came to the attention of the press for his controversial performance during the "New York Battle" of *Iron Chef*. Six months later, in January 2001, he would get his chance to avenge his loss to Masaharu Morimoto.

FLAY VS. MORIMOTO, ROUND 2

An *Iron Chef* rematch was scheduled for Flay and Morimoto, but this battle took place in Tokyo, Japan. Dubbed the "21st Century Battle," the cooking competition was held in the same studio—the Kitchen Stadium—in which Fuji TV's *Iron Chef* was filmed. In interviews, Flay had indicated that he was still troubled by Morimoto's response to his actions at the end of their last meeting. It had never been his intention to disrespect the famed chef, he said.

The show began with the two competitors being introduced by Chairman Takeshi Kaga. The secret ingredient was then unveiled: 60 Japanese lobsters that Kaga said were valued at $10,000. He gave the signal for the match to begin, and Flay and Morimoto set to work.

Both chefs entered the competition with definite plans. Morimoto had decided that he would not use soy sauce, one of the most common condiments in Japanese cooking. He soaked his lobsters in sake and prepared dishes using, among other things, Gorgonzola cheese, white truffles, and caviar. Flay was determined to use his signature ingredients. "The one thing I decided early on," he told *New York Daily News*,

The Food Network divides its programming into daytime and nighttime categories. Daytime programs are largely how-to cooking shows. Nighttime programs offer other food-related shows and competitions.

"was that I was not going to put anything Japanese or Asian in my cooking. . . . I was going to cook within myself, and use ingredients and dishes that I've been used to making for the last 20 years." He prepared dishes using Kobe beef, horseradish, and blue corn, as well as his signature blend of spices.

When time was called, Bobby once again jumped up on the countertop in a premature victory celebration. This time, however, to avoid showing any disrespect to his opponent, he first tossed the cutting board on the floor.

The judges included a food critic, an actor, a retired sumo wrestler, and an officer from the U.S. Embassy. They were impressed with both chefs' dishes, and their comments seemed to favor Morimoto. When the marks were totaled, however, Flay was pronounced the winner by a score of 89 to 83.

Bobby and Morimoto pose together at a cooking event. The two chefs have waged several notable battles in "kitchen stadium" over the years.

BOY MEETS GRILL

In 2002 Flay debuted another new show for the Food Network, called *Boy Meets Grill*. Although the show would become a personal favorite, when it was first proposed to him, he hesitated to sign on. He didn't want to do another grilling show, he said, but he was willing if the setting would be in New York. He explained:

> I'm from New York. . . . I want to shoot a grilling show in New York City, and I want New York City to be my backdrop. . . . And I want to shop in New York, I want to procure the food in New York, every borough. And then I want to bring it back to a rooftop somewhere and have the 59th Street Bridge in the background.

The Food Network agreed to Bobby's demands. But the desire to shoot on a Long Island City rooftop in the July heat would be difficult. The first day of filming, it was 110 degrees in the shade. And Bobby was working a hot grill for seven hours at a time.

Despite the complications the show was a big success. *Boy Meets Grill* was nominated for an Emmy for Outstanding Service Show in 2004. Bobby won as the year's Outstanding Service Show Host in 2005.

Flay also appeared in specials for the Food Network. *Tasting Ireland*, which aired in 2003, had special meaning for him. In it the red-haired chef traveled to the Emerald Isle,

Marinating a piece of meat before grilling it adds flavor to it. It also moistens the surface of the meat and helps prevent it from drying out when it is grilled.

the home of his ancestors. There, he sampled the foods of Ireland and visited several of the thousands of pubs that dot the country. Recipes for native dishes such as dingle pie and boxty pancakes were included in the show.

THE GRILL-MEISTER

Flay was best known, however, for his grilling shows. The popularity of *Grillin' and Chillin'*, *Hot Off the Grill with Bobby Flay*, and *Boy Meets Grill* led to other Food Network shows showcasing his grilling skills. *BBQ with Bobby Flay* and *Grill It! with Bobby Flay* both proved popular with outdoor cooking enthusiasts.

THE COOKING CHANNEL

In May 2010 Scripps Networks Interactive, owners of the Food Network, launched a spin-off network, the Cooking Channel. The new network focused on information and instructional programs instead of featuring the competition-based shows found on the Food Network.

The Cooking Channel features programs hosted by celebrity chefs Bobby Flay, Emeril Lagasse, Rachael Ray, and many others. In 2011 these shows included:

- *Food Jammers*: Unusual food contraptions like a taco vending machine.
- *Chinese Food Made Easy*: Easy, quick-to-make Chinese recipes.
- *Food(ography)*: An informational food show hosted by humorist Mo Rocca.
- *Unique Eats*: A look at some of today's most unusual foods and restaurants.
- *Spice Goddess*: Indian meals made with wholesome ingredients and fresh herbs and spices.

BBQ with Bobby Flay debuted in 2004. As host of the travelogue show, Bobby traveled around the country visiting restaurants, grills, and cook-offs. He exchanged tips with local grilling experts and sampled the barbeque specialties of each region.

Grill It! with Bobby Flay premiered in 2008. The show gave Food Network viewers a chance to grill alongside their favorite chef. Aspiring cooks would submit videos of themselves preparing their favorite recipes. Some of them would be chosen to appear on the show and prepare their recipe. In a gimmick similar to the one used on *Iron Chef*, that basic ingredient of the guest's dish would be kept secret from Bobby. He would not know what the food was until the guest chef arrived. He would then come up with his own recipe using that particular ingredient.

Bobby has said that he loves the festive atmosphere associated with grilling, the way it makes entertaining at home less formal, and the way it reminds people of their childhood. But as much as he loves it, he admits that "grilling is not really the most passionate thing for me. The reason why I got stuck with the grilling thing is that I did . . . *Grillin' and Chillin'*, so now I'm a grilling expert."

The host of *Chef's Story*, French Culinary Institute founder and CEO Dorothy Cann Hamilton, considers Bobby's name to be synonymous with grilling. She once introduced him on the show as "the most famous grill-meister since Satan."

COOKBOOKS TO GRILL BY

Bobby's successful grilling shows and the demand for his recipes motivated him to add four more cookbooks to his résumé. *Bobby Flay's Boy Meets Grill* (1999), *Bobby Flay's Boy Gets Grill* (2004), *Bobby Flay's Grilling For Life* (2005), and *Bobby Flay's Grill It!* (2008) all met with success in book-stores across the country.

The recipes in the cookbooks reflect Flay's creativity and passion for using bold flavors when cooking over a fire. Most people think of beef as the basic food for grilling. But as his recipes reveal, Bobby believes that just about anything can be grilled—these foods include beef, chicken, lamb, turkey, fish, shellfish, vegetables, and fruits. Even soups and salads can be partially prepared on a grill, he says. He did admit to an interviewer that there was one food he couldn't cook on a grill—scrambled eggs. "I tried to grill scrambled eggs," he said. "But . . . it doesn't work. I thought about the quickest-cooking thing in the world, so I thought if I got the heat high enough the grates would grab it and they would start cooking in the air. But basically I scrambled the eggs and they went right through the grates—never to be seen again." Bobby would have better luck with other projects.

Thanks to his television shows and cookbooks, Bobby is widely recognized as an expert on grilling food.

CHAPTER SIX

MORE CHALLENGES

For many years Flay was content with running his successful restaurants—Mesa Grill and Bolo—in New York. He felt comfortable cooking for New Yorkers and had no particular desire to expand his territory beyond his home borough of Manhattan. However, that attitude eventually changed.

LAS VEGAS

Bobby's New York restaurants enjoyed widespread popularity and success, and he often received offers to bring his cuisine to other parts of the country. Until 2003 he had always refused these offers. He preferred to remain based in New York City, where he could easily spend time with his young daughter, who lived there. And he did not relish the changes in lifestyle that a move would entail.

But in 2003 Bobby received a proposal from Caesars Palace in Las Vegas, Nevada, to open a new Bolo restaurant in the popular gambling capital. Flay felt the time was right to expand his restaurants, but he decided that a new Mesa

Grill would be a better choice for his first restaurant outside New York City. In announcing the agreement in early 2004, Caesars Palace president Mark Juliano said, "Bobby Flay's new Mesa Grill will be a stand-alone destination for Las Vegas and a wonderful addition to the dining array at Caesars Palace. In addition to Flay's formidable culinary talent, his team consistently provides an elevated atmosphere of warm hospitality."

The new Mesa Grill would be part of the Caesars Palace Hotel and Casino complex, which includes several restaurants. This meant that Bobby and his partners—Jerry Kretchmer, Laurence Kretchmer, and Jeff Bliss—would not have complete control of the restaurant as they did at Mesa Grill and Bolo in New York. To ensure that the food served at the new venue matched the quality of his original restaurant, Bobby moved seven chefs who were familiar with Flay's cuisine, together with their families, to Las Vegas. The move held a bonus in that they went from overpriced apartments in New York City to several-bedroom homes in Las Vegas.

Sign at the entrance to Bobby's Mesa Grill at Caesars restaurant.

Mesa Grill at Caesars opened in October 2004. Designed by David Rockwell, a well-known interior architect, the restaurant featured a massive 20-foot-tall rotisserie, with a grill and quesadilla oven. The Food Network

ENTERTAINMENT CAPITAL OF THE WORLD

Bobby's first restaurant venture outside New York took him to Las Vegas, a city that is famous as a gaming and gambling center. Home to numerous casino resorts, it has long had the reputation of being the entertainment capital of the world.

Established in 1905, Las Vegas served as a railroad hub in the early 1900s. The town grew rapidly and by 1911 it was incorporated as a city. In 1935, when nearby Hoover Dam was completed, Las Vegas experienced a surge in growth. However, it was the legalization of gambling earlier in the decade that would give the city its claim to fame.

After gambling became legal in 1931, organized crime funded the construction of casino resorts that attracted tourists from around the country. The mob was eventually run out of Las Vegas in the 1960s.

In recent years, the city has become more of a family-oriented destination. Today, with a population of approximately 2 million, Las Vegas has earned the distinction of being the most populous American city founded in the 20th century.

Caesar's Palace, where Bobby opened a second Mesa Grill in 2004, is on the left in this photo of the Las Vegas strip.

filmed the design, construction, and opening of the new restaurant. The resulting program was broadcast in January 2005 as a television special called *Bobby's Vegas Gamble*.

LOVE AND MARRIAGE

In the early 2000s Bobby also made some changes in his personal life. In March 2001 an acquaintance of Flay's, the actress Mariska Hargitay, set him up on a blind date with actress Stephanie March. Hargitay was the star of the hit series *Law & Order: Special Victims Unit*. Stephanie played the role of Assistant District Attorney Alexandra Cabot on the show.

Bobby and Stephanie's first date was at Nobu, a popular Japanese restaurant in New York. The couple hit it off and began dating on a regular basis. As Bobby was working out the details on his Las Vegas restaurant, he was also making decisions about the relationship. In December 2004, during a skating date at the ice rink at Rockefeller Center, he asked Stephanie to marry him. She accepted, and the couple married on February 20, 2005, exactly four years after their first date.

TV ACTOR

While Stephanie and Bobby were dating, she made several guest appearances on his Food Network shows. In 2005 Bobby appeared on her show, with a role in an episode of *Law & Order: Special Victims Unit*. In a classic example of typecasting, he played the part of a chef.

Flay already had a bit of acting experience before appearing in *Law & Order*. In 2003 he had a cameo role as himself in the Disney Channel movie *Eddie's Million Dollar Cook-Off*. Bobby has downplayed his acting ability. He says he is

Bobby and Stephanie March Flay leave the church after their February 2005 wedding. Stephanie, a successful television and film actress, has also appeared as a guest judge on several of Bobby's Food Network shows.

better suited for the role of a chef at his restaurants and on the Food Network.

IRON CHEF AMERICA

In late 2004 viewers saw Flay in a Food Network miniseries special called *Iron Chef America: Battle of the Masters*. It was a spinoff of the Japanese program *Iron Chef*. The American version featured two original *Iron Chef* cooks, Hiroyuki Sakai and Masharu Morimoto, facing off against Food Network American chefs Bobby Flay, Mario Batali, and Wolfgang Puck.

The first competition, in which Flay competed against Sakai, featured trout as the secret ingredient. A highlight of that battle was Sakai's creation of trout ice cream, which would become part of *Iron Chef* lore. Other competitions saw Morimoto take on Batali, and then clash with Puck. The final battle of the competition saw former foes Flay and Morimoto team up to defeat Batali and Sakai.

Cat Cora was the first woman to serve as an Iron Chef. She has appeared on Iron Chef America *since 2005.*

When it aired in late 2004 the special garnered high ratings. The following January the new series *Iron Chef America* premiered. The program featured three Iron Chefs facing off against challenger chefs. Bobby starred as one of the three Iron Chefs. The other two with Batali and Morimoto. Other Iron Chefs who have appeared on the show include Cat Cora, Jose Garces, Michel Symon, and Marc Forgione.

Over the years Bobby has taken part in many *Iron Chef America* competitions. In November 2006 he participated in "Battle Cranberry," and partnered with Food Network personality Giada De Laurentiis in a matchup against Rachael Ray and Batali. Ray and Batali emerged victorious in what would be one of the highest-rated shows ever broadcast on the Food Network.

Two years later "Thanksgiving Showdown" matched two Iron Chef teams: Flay and Michael Symon competed against Morimoto and Cat Cora. The secret ingredients for this competition were foods that might have been used at the first Thanksgiving celebration, such as duck, turkey, corn, and walnuts. This time Bobby's team came out on top, winning the competition.

Like Bobby Flay, Giada De Laurentiis is a popular Food Network star. She has hosted several hit shows, including Everyday Italian *and* Giada at Home, *and teamed up with Bobby for a 2006* Iron Chef America *battle.*

In November 2009 Flay faced off against Morimoto once again in the *Iron Chef America* "Holiday Ice Battle." In this last episode of the show's seventh season, the team of Morimoto and Takeo Okamoto defeated partners Flay and Shintaro Okamoto.

In 2007 Bobby had a hand in a spin-off of *Iron Chef America*. The new show was a competition among a group of chefs for the honor of appearing as an Iron Chef on *Iron Chef America*. Bobby served on *The Next Iron Chef* panel of judges that determined which contestants qualify for the honor. The show debuted in 2007.

BAR AMERICAIN

Flay's restaurants were keeping him busy. And after more than a decade of serving Southwestern cuisine at Mesa Grill and Spanish food at Bolo, Bobby wanted his next eatery to take a different approach. In April 2005 he opened Bar Americain on West 52nd Street in Manhattan. One of its chefs, Neil Manacle, explained the meaning of the restaurant's name. "In Paris," he said, "this meant that the bar served American style cocktails. This was geared for the tourists and even for the French. . . . So we were looking through a cookbook and saw a picture with 'Bar Americain' written on it and thought that an American style brasserie would be a hit here in the city."

The Bar Americain menu featured regional fare, highlighting the kinds of food Bobby encountered in various parts of the United States while filming *FoodNation*. Among the entrees were Florida-style red snapper, smoked trout from the Carolinas, and artisanal ham from Kentucky and Georgia. Bobby developed dishes such as crispy squash blossoms stuffed with pulled pork and ricotta in a black pepper vinegar sauce.

Like Mesa Grill and Bolo, Bar Americain received posi-

The first *Iron Chef* spinoff, called *Iron Chef USA*, aired in late 2001 on the UPN network. Hosted by actor William Shatner, the ill-fated show lasted only two episodes. Bobby had no affiliation with *Iron Chef USA*.

tive reviews from the critics. *The New York Times* awarded it two stars, and the eatery quickly became a favorite of New York diners.

TAKING CARE OF BUSINESS

Running a restaurant is not an easy thing to do. While his partners run the business end, Flay maintains charge of the kitchens, and he pays attention to every single detail. In an interview, Bobby described one of his sample days:

> Every restaurant gets four big changes a year, and . . . this week [the changes are] at Bar Americain. . . . On Monday, we're doing all the appetizers, including the new ones for the season, and I'm training the cooks, we're cooking them, we're hopefully perfecting them. . . . And then I'm serving them to the entire staff. It's a mandatory meeting where the bartenders, the bus-boys, the waiters, the managers, everybody in the restaurant must come, and they must eat the food, and I sit there and I tell them about it. And I tell them why we're serving it on the menu . . . so that they have a story and they know that it's not just shrimp on a plate.

THROWDOWN! WITH BOBBY FLAY

In between running his restaurants, Bobby found time to develop another Food Network show, *Throwdown! with Bobby Flay*. On each show, the celebrity chef throws down a challenge to a local chef or cook who is known for a particular dish. The food might be something simple, like hamburgers or chocolate chip cookies. Or it could be something more unusual, such as the Indian dish chicken tikka masala or the Yule log cake called Bûche de Noël.

A key part of *Throwdown!* is that the local chef or cook is unaware that Bobby is setting up a challenge. The chef is simply told that he or she is going to be the subject of a segment on a new Food Network show. As part of this show, the cook is asked to hold a small party. During the party Bobby appears, reveals the ruse, and challenges the subject to a throwdown, that is, a cook-off competition of their specialty. After Flay and the featured chef prepare the same signature dish, they have their work evaluated by a pair of local judges, and a winner is announced.

As part of the show, the cameras follow Bobby and his two assistants, Stephanie Banyas and Miriam Garron, as they research the dish and experiment with variations. In an article published by Reuters, Bobby explained:

> Stephanie, Miriam and I sort of conference. . . .They do the research and I drive what the flavor profile would be. We just go to the kitchen and mess around a little bit. We don't try to perfect it in there. We just get used to the technique or the ingredients. There are certain ingredients and flavors I'm more gravitated toward so it sort of has my signature on it.

Throwdown! with Bobby Flay premiered in July 2006 and soon became one of the Food Network's most popular shows.

Some viewers have criticized the program. They say that Flay is attempting to belittle local chefs by beating them at their specialty. He strongly disagrees. Bobby believes the show provides a win-win situation for everyone involved. Even if they lose, competitors still get national exposure for themselves and their food. "*Throwdown!* really is not about winning or losing," he says. "It's about showcasing these people more than anything else." The results back him up: Bobby

When Bobby first proposed the idea for *Throwdown!* to the Food Network, he did not want a panel of judges to declare a winner. Instead, he wanted the program to end with clips shown of people eating the two dishes and making comments. This would allow the viewers to decide for themselves who won.

has lost more than twice as often as he has won. His record at the end of the program's eighth season, after 101 episodes, was 32 wins, 68 losses, and 1 tie.

THE NEXT FOOD NETWORK STAR

Flay has said that he considers the Food Network his television home. So it followed that he would become involved in a television competition that selects chef hosts for the network. On *The Next Food Network Star*, Bobby helps judge chefs who are competing for the chance to win a six-show contract to host a television program.

When judging the contestants on the reality show, Bobby looks for three things in particular. "They need to be able to cook with authority," he told *Eclipse Magazine*, "they need to be able to be a good teacher and be able to inspire, and if they have these two things they need to be entertaining. You have to be able to hold the viewer." Bobby could easily say that those are requirements that he himself fits.

RAW TALENT

RARE OPPORTUNITY

WELL D[O]

As a judge on the popular show The Next Food
Network Star, Bobby has helped to identify several
up-and-coming talents for the network, including
Aaron McCargo (Big Daddy's House) and Melissa
d'Arabian (Ten Dollar Dinners). Bobby is pictured
here with contestants from the show's fifth season.

CHAPTER SEVEN

AN EXPANDING EMPIRE

A well-known sports adage is that it is difficult to get to the top, but even harder to stay there. The same holds true in the culinary field. It is important to maintain a level of excellence in restaurants because it can take only one bad experience to turn a regular customer at a restaurant into one who never returns.

During the first decade of 2000 Bobby continued to stay on top. His original restaurants as well as the new eateries he opened consistently got glowing reviews. At the same time, he produced numerous cookbooks and made a name for himself on national television.

BOBBY FLAY STEAK

In June 2006 the celebrity chef opened another restaurant outside New York City. Bobby Flay Steak was located at the Borgata Hotel Casino and Spa, in Atlantic City, New Jersey. It was Flay's first steakhouse. Classic steak dishes and restaurant entrees inspired by Bobby's memories of his childhood in New York and at the Jersey shore appeared on the menu. Many dishes featured Flay's distinctive signature spicy rubs and southwestern seasonings.

When asked why he selected Atlantic City as the location for the restaurant, Bobby explained,

> First and foremost I consider Bobby Flay Steak a surf and turf restaurant. . . . If you remember Atlantic City in its original heyday . . . all the restaurants along the water served their version of surf and turf. Obviously at Bobby Flay Steak we're doing a much more contemporary version of that. Whenever I do a restaurant I think about the location and sense of place.

BOBBY'S BURGER PALACE

Flay's first restaurants were all high-end establishments. That is, they were expensive, sophisticated eateries aimed at business people or couples out for a night on the town. Bobby planned that his next culinary undertaking would provide a more casual dining experience. In July 2008 he opened Bobby's Burger Palace in the village of Lake Grove, on Long Island, New York.

Bobby's Burger Palace was also a tribute to one of the celebrity chef's favorite foods. Flay has often said that he likes to eat cheeseburgers. But in developing his burger restaurant, he took the concept to the next level. The menu lists the basic beef patty but with variations inspired by Flay's travels around the country. The L.A. Burger is topped with avocado relish, watercress, cheddar cheese, and tomato. The Philadelphia Burger is adorned with provolone cheese, grilled onions, and hot peppers. And the spice-crusted Dallas Burger is garnished with coleslaw, Monterey Jack cheese, barbeque sauce, and pickles. Specialty burgers are also intro-

Gourmet Hamburgers

Other celebrity chefs besides Bobby have opened restaurants that serve the all-American sandwich, the hamburger. Emeril Lagasse opened Burgers and More, Marcus Samuelsson created Marc Burger, and Laurent Tourondel founded LT Burger. Hamburgers are also often found on the menus of many upscale restaurants.

High-end burgers differ in many ways from the fast food variety. Some may be made using high quality meats, such as Kobe or Angus beef, and from cuts such as short rib, sirloin, or brisket. Many gourmet eateries feature burgers made of turkey, lamb, and even salmon. Specialty breads such as artisanal rolls and brioches have replaced the traditional sesame-seed hamburger bun.

The typical garnishes of American cheese, pickles, and ketchup seldom appear on upscale burgers. Instead, they are adorned with gourmet cheeses, avocados, pineapples, and Portobello mushrooms. Homemade ketchups, mustards, relishes, chilies, and salsas are the rule rather than the exception.

Gourmet hamburgers may range in price from $8 to $25. And it is possible to spend much more. In 2008 the Fleur de Lys restaurant in Las Vegas made news when it offered a luxury burger for $5,000. The FleurBurger was made with Kobe beef, garnished with black truffles and foie gras, and came accompanied by a bottle of 1990 Chateau Petrus wine.

Bobby Flay's gourmet burgers are made with Angus beef, ground turkey, or chicken breast.

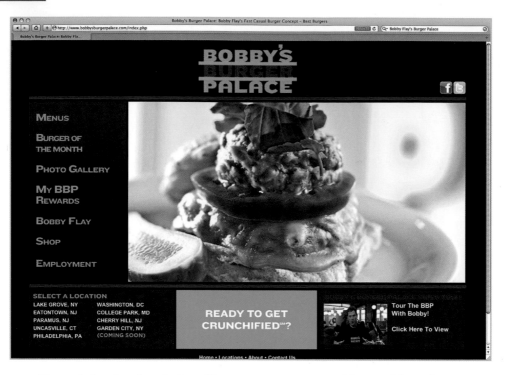

The website for the chain of burger restaurants Bobby established in 2008. Today there are nine Bobby's Burger Palace restaurants; they are located in the northeastern United States.

duced at regular intervals. All of the burgers can be "crunchified" with a thick layer of potato chips for added texture.

Turkey or chicken breast burgers are also offered at Bobby's Burger Palace. Diners looking to avoid meat altogether can opt for a griddled cheese sandwich or a crunch salad. And as in any burger restaurant, French fries and onion rings are offered.

The restaurant on Long Island was such a success that Flay began to expand the franchise. From 2008 to 2010 he opened other Bobby's Burger Palace restaurants in locations such as Eatontown and Paramus, New Jersey, and Philadelphia, Pennsylvania. He also opened one in the Mohegan Sun Casino in Uncasville, Connecticut.

A WAGE DIFFERENCE OF OPINION

In early 2009 Flay was also dealing with serious legal issues. Many New York City restaurant owners had come under scrutiny for possible violations of labor laws that regulated wages, tips, and overtime. Over the past few years, a wave of lawsuits had hit some of the major names in the culinary world, including Bobby's Food Network colleagues Mario Batali and Masaharu Morimoto.

Plaintiffs sued restaurant owners over what they contended were illegal wage practices such as forcing staff to share tips with managers and other ineligible employees, failure to properly pay overtime, and failure to reimburse employees for required expenses. The owners blamed the problem on confusing wage and hour regulations in the Fair Labor Standards Act and New York Labor Law. Some critics claimed a few lawyers seeking publicity were bringing the lawsuits. They cited one lawyer who had filed more than 100 such suits. Others acknowledged that such practices have been around for a long time.

In January 2009 Bobby's company, Bold Foods LLC, was named in a lawsuit brought by former employees at his restaurants. He eventually settled, agreeing to pay over $800,000 to settle claims. But he denied any wrongdoing.

Many defendants in similar lawsuits settled out of court, while affirming innocence, because a loss in court could result in much more severe penalties. Although settling lawsuits in this manner presented the appearance of admitting guilt, in this situation, it did not seem likely that the restaurant owners were all guilty. Tim and Nina Zagat noted in the *New York Times*, "It defies common sense to think that so many of the city's most respected restaurateurs have intentionally cheated their waiters—and continue to do so despite the threat of costly lawsuits that could drive them out of business."

Some legal analysts believe that the number of lawsuits in New York will shrink in the future because of the state's Hospitality Wage Order, which went into effect in January 2011. The order requires restaurants to be more attentive to how they pay their workers.

TAKING TO THE AIRWAVES

Around the same time his company was hit with the lawsuit, Flay debuted a radio program, *Bobby Flay Radio*. He hosted the two-hour-a-day program on the Sirius XM satellite radio network. The call-in show was Bobby's idea, and Sirius was only too happy to accommodate him. In announcing the new program, Jeremy Coleman, vice president of Talk, Information and Entertainment Programming at Sirius praised Bobby, saying, "His natural style, humor and ability to inform and entertain make him the perfect fit for SIRIUS XM. *Bobby Flay Radio* is an exciting new venture for us and for his millions of fans."

On the show Bobby offered lifestyle advice for men on topics ranging from food to dating to fashion. His wife, Stephanie, occasionally joined him, and provided tips from a woman's perspective. Another regular was Bobby's friend and sports consultant "Larry K," who made predictions and led discussions on topics related to sports. The program ran for five weeks, ending its run in February 2009.

A SURPRISE INVITATION

The following June Bobby was scheduled to make an appearance at the Food and Wine Classic in Aspen, Colorado. But at the last minute his plans had to be adjusted when he

Bobby has said that grilling steaks and chicken with President Barack Obama at the White House was a highlight of his professional career. He said afterward that the main piece of advice he gave the president was not to turn the steaks too soon.

received an invitation he couldn't refuse. He was invited to Washington, D.C., to take part in President Barack Obama's Father's Day event, being held a few days before the Sunday holiday. Flay was invited to join the Friday afternoon barbeque honoring mentors and father figures for young people. The crowd included male teenagers and their mentors, who included military officers, celebrity chefs, professional athletes, and college presidents.

As part of the activities, Bobby manned the grill, where he barbequed steaks and burgers. At one point President Obama joined him, and the pair cooked together for about 20 minutes. During that time Bobby offered the president some grilling tips.

Upon completion of the festivities, Bobby hopped on a plane and flew to Aspen in time to give a cooking demonstration the next day. He later told the *Los Angeles Times*, "Cooking at the White House . . . was probably my greatest professional moment."

MOHEGAN SUN

Later in the year Bobby got back to the task at hand: preparing for the opening of another upscale eatery. On November 18, 2009, less than five months after opening Bobby's Burger Palace at Mohegan Sun, Flay opened a new Bar Americain at the same venue.

Like the original Bar Americain, the new restaurant celebrated regional foods and specialties found in various parts of

Located along the banks of the Thames River in Uncasville, Connecticut, Mohegan Sun is the second-largest casino in the United States. It was developed in partnership with the Mohegan tribe and opened to the public in 1996. Mohegan Sun is home to more than 40 restaurants and food and beverage outlets, including two affiliated with Bobby Flay.

the United States. In honor of its location, it featured dishes showcasing the ingredients natural to New England.

The Mohegan Sun Casino was developed in partnership with the Mohegan tribe and its décor reflects this Native American heritage. For the restaurant Bobby developed a Native American theme dish featuring fry bread. A kind of Native American taco, the bread was filled with barbequed duck and cranberry red chilies.

Super Chef Battle

The year 2010 started with a bang for Bobby. On January 3 the Food Network broadcast a two-hour episode of *Iron Chef America* called "Super Chef Battle." The special was taped at the White House in Washington, D.C., and at the Iron Chef America Kitchen Stadium in New York City. The show starred celebrity chefs Iron Chefs Bobby Flay and Mario Batali, and super chefs Emeril Lagasse and Cristeta Comerford.

The first part of the program featured first lady Michelle Obama. She welcomed Flay, Batali, and Lagasse to the White House and talked about its fruit and vegetable garden. One of Michelle Obama's first acts after moving into the White House in January 2009 was the creation of a garden in a corner of the South Lawn. The garden was used to help teach kids about healthy eating, and its produce became a staple at White House dinners. In addition, more than 1,000 pounds of fruit and vegetables from the garden were donated that year to charitable causes.

Michelle then revealed that the secret ingredient for the upcoming *Iron Chef America* competition was anything from the White House garden. This segment was filmed late in 2009, so the garden featured fall and winter crops such as

In February 2010 Michelle Obama introduced the Let's Move! Initiative. It is a program to reduce childhood obesity by promoting healthy eating, encouraging kids to exercise, and supporting the use of local foods from farmers' markets and community gardens.

collard greens, kale, fennel, broccoli, rhubarb, icicle radish, purple cauliflower, eggplant, kohlrabi, and watermelon. The chefs were also told that they could use honey from the White House beehives.

Batali and Lagasse were informed that they would be one team. Bobby was paired with Comerford, who is the White House executive chef. She had worked at the White House since 1995, at first as an assistant chef during Bill Clinton's administration. In 2005 First Lady Laura Bush promoted Comerford to the position of executive chef. Michelle Obama reappointed her four years later.

Filming shifted next to the Iron Chef Kitchen Stadium in New York City, where the competition took place. Since almost a week had passed since the Washington, D.C., segment was shot, the vegetables and fruits the chefs harvested from the White House garden were not used. They were replaced with locally grown produce.

Each side had to prepare five dishes within the allotted hour. Judges would evaluate the chefs' efforts and give points based on categories of taste, plating, and originality. Serving as judges for the event were chef Nigella Lawson, actress Jane Seymour, and Olympic swimmer Natalie Coughlin. The team awarded the highest score would win $25,000 for the charity of their choice.

(Above) First Lady Michelle Obama and her daughters harvest fall vegetables from the White House kitchen garden, accompanied by chefs and elementary school students. (Right) White House Executive Chef Cristeta "Cris" Comerford teamed up with Bobby to win a 2009 Iron Chef America competition filmed at the White House.

At the end of the hour, both sides were ready. The Batali and Lagasse dishes consisted of a scallop, radish, and fennel salad; an oyster and salad trio; sweet potato and cheese ravioli; a quail and turkey duet; and heirloom carrot beignets. Flay and Comerford countered with an oyster, fennel, and apple salad; a garden salad with lobster and squid; broccoli clam chowder; a barbeque with pork and a collard green tamale; and a meringue sweet potato tart.

The judge's votes were tabulated: The two teams tied in the taste category, but Flay and Comerford won in presentation and originality. With a score of 55 to 50, they prevailed over Batali and Lagasse. The big winner was the organization

Citymeals-on-Wheels, which received the $25,000 donation from the Food Network.

BRUNCH @ BOBBY'S

In May 2010 Flay began hosting another new show, this time on a new cable television network, the Cooking Channel. It started up that month as a spinoff of the Food Network.

Brunch @ Bobby's featured many of Flay's recipes for dishes to be served at brunch, which he calls his favorite meal of the day. The program is instructional, with Flay teaching viewers how to make specific dishes. He also gives viewers tips and tricks they can apply in their own cooking.

AMERICA'S NEXT GREAT RESTAURANT

Bobby's next television venture offered a change of pace from his other shows. For one thing, it was broadcast over network television—NBC—rather than the Food Network. The show was *America's Next Great Restaurant*. It made its debut in March 2011.

America's Next Great Restaurant was a reality show in which contestants vied for the chance to fulfill their dream of opening a restaurant. The first season began with 21 contestants who pitched their ideas and concepts for a new chain of eateries. The top 10 then took part in a series of weekly competitions based on various aspects of the restaurant business. Challenges included preparing signature dishes and designing uniform logos and restaurant interiors.

Bobby hosted the program and served as one of its four judges. The three other judges were restaurateurs Steve Ells, Lorena Garcia, and Curtis Stone. The four also mentored the contestants by providing advice and support.

The winner of *America's Next Great Restaurant* had much

more to gain than just a brief moment of television fame. He or she would receive financial backing to open up three restaurants—in Los Angeles, Minneapolis, and New York City—based on the winning idea. As investors in the restaurants, Flay, Ells, Garcia, and Stone had a financial stake in the outcome of the show.

Bobby liked the program's concept. "I think that's part of the brilliance of the show," he said in an interview. "I think that, because we are investors, we have this vested interest in making sure that the person who wins really is going to be successful, as opposed to, you know, a reality show where there's a prize and then that's it." Unfortunately, the show did not attract many viewers, and it was cancelled after its first season ended in May.

Meanwhile, Bobby was opening more of his own restaurants. In late 2010 he had announced plans to launch more Bobby's Burger Palace restaurants along the East Coast. One opened in Washington, D.C., in August 2011 and another in College Park, Maryland, the following October.

BOBBY FLAY PRODUCTS

Like several of today's celebrity chefs, Flay markets a line of his distinctive marinades, sauces and salsas. His gourmet foods are available for purchase online and in stores. The bestsellers include Bobby Flay Steak Sauce, Bobby Flay Steak Rub, Mesa Grill 16 Spice Poultry Rub, Mesa Grill Jalapeno Hot Sauce, and Mesa Grill Habanero Mango Hot Sauce.

In 2007 Bobby expanded his brand by entering into an agreement to sell cookware, dinnerware, grilling tools, and other cooking merchandise that carry his name. These products are sold exclusively at Kohl's department stores.

Thanks to his charming smile and confident presence, Bobby has become one of the most popular celebrity chefs on the Food Network.

CHAPTER EIGHT

UP CLOSE AND PERSONAL

Although busy with the responsibilities of a bestselling author and TV personality, Flay has said he still considers his highest priority to be his restaurants. He spends a great deal of his time in his restaurant kitchens and overseeing business operations. Despite this heavy workload, he also makes time for his family and hobbies. In fact, he escapes the pressures that go with being a public figure by spending time with his family and doing the things he enjoys. And he also tries to give back to the field that brought him fame and fortune.

BAD BOY REPUTATION

Flay is one of the most popular personalities on the Food Network. His legion of fans and admirers eagerly follow his every move on the cooking landscape.

But like most people in the public eye, Bobby has his share of detractors. He has confidence in his abilities and carries himself with an assurance that some people interpret as arrogance. He has even been referred to as the "culinary bad boy," especially early in his television career, because of his sometimes abrasive behavior onscreen. In 2007 the culinary director at Bold Foods, Christine Sanchez, defended her boss. "People need a label," she told *Franchise Times*. "I don't know how that got started. People are surprised he's so warm and approachable."

For some people, their negative feelings about Flay date back to his controversial antics at the end of the *Iron Chef* "Battle New York" against Masaharu Morimoto. They disapproved of his complaints during the competition and viewed his jumping up on the table and premature celebration as a sign of arrogance and immaturity.

Bobby acknowledges his behavior have changed since his early years as a chef. In an interview aired on *Chef's Story*, he explained:

> When I opened Mesa Grill, I was twenty-five years old and sort of not quite broken. . . . I had a lot going on at a very young age. And so I think that what happened was that I didn't really sort of stop long enough to understand how what you say can affect certain people. . . . I think as I got a little bit more mature and sort of mellowed a little bit, I just realized that . . . the fact is that it's a lot more satisfying to be nicer to people.

Bobby also has critics who say he spends too much time in front of the camera, and as a result has little time to spend in his restaurants. Flay responds that the filming does not take very long—he has been known to film a whole season in six days. But because the shows are broadcast more than once, it seems like he is continuously on television. He points out that on cable, they "shoot a little and show it a lot."

CHEF'S DREAM HOUSE

Bobby's success as a chef, cookbook author, and television personality gave him the financial ability to build the house of his dreams. After living in Manhattan his entire life, he moved to a new home in the South Shore of Long Island in 2010.

Bobby and Stephanie began building the house in October 2009 in Amagansett, a community in the town of East Hampton. The couple built with hopes of having the home certified as a green home by Leadership in Energy and Environmental Design (LEED). Such certification means that the building was designed and constructed with practices intended for good environmental and health performance.

Bobby explained that an environmentally sound home was important to Stephanie. "She said to me, 'I'm not building this house unless we're incredibly thoughtful about it,'" he told *Hamptons Magazine*. "People talk about green this and green that, but really, it just comes down to what's right and what's common sense."

Construction of the house, which is located in a wooded area, was completed the following year. According to Bobby, the new home has only one extravagance. As befits a chef, that extravagance is the kitchens.

There are two fully functioning kitchens—one inside and one outside. One of the indoor kitchen's amenities is a deep fryer, while the outdoor kitchen features a brick pizza oven, charcoal grill, and refrigeration system. Flay explained,

Bobby Flay is a master instructor and visiting chef at the French Culinary Institute.

"Inside it's like a little French café, with a giant marble island and a café area with some tables and rattan chairs. Then you walk through a big door into the outdoor kitchen area. When it's all open, you feel like you're walking through a restaurant."

A PASSION FOR HORSES

Another benefit of Bobby's successful career is that he has the funds to indulge in his hobby of horse racing. He has said that his earliest memory of visiting a racetrack was a trip to Belmont Park on Long Island with his grandfather, Willie Flay, when he was just 12 years old. That early interest in horse racing led him to become an owner and breeder of several racehorses through his company B. Flay Thoroughbreds, Inc.

One of Bobby's first ventures in buying a racehorse was as a partner with John Phillips and Richard Santulli. Their mare, Wonder Again, competed in the 2005 Breeders' Cup Filly and Mare Turf, finishing fourth. Together with his partners, Bobby also purchased the thoroughbreds Unbridled Express and Gilded Gold. His other horses include Mesa Girl, Grace and Power, and Sophie's Salad, named for his daughter.

Flay admits to being totally immersed in horseracing. He has said that when he has trouble sleeping at night, he sometimes watches replays of races and reads pedigrees.

In 2010 Bobby's horse More Than Real scored an upset victory over the heavily favored Winter Memories in the

Bobby Flay bought his first racehorse, named Sophie's Salad, around 2004. Sophie's chopped salad is also a popular dish at Bobby's Mesa Grill restaurants.

Bobby leads his filly Her Smile, carrying jockey Javier Castellano, to the winner's circle after the horse captured the Prioress Stakes, a Grade 1 horse race, at Belmont Park in New York on July 4, 2011. The horse would go on to finish third in the 2011 Breeders' Cup Filly and Mare Sprint race.

Breeders' Cup Juvenile Fillies Turf, held at the Churchill Downs racetrack in Kentucky. The victory provided him with his first Breeders' Cup win and was the highlight of his career as a thoroughbred owner.

STILL ENJOYING SPORTS

Although his dreams of a career as a professional athlete ended in high school, Flay stays in shape by continuing to exercise. At one time he played basketball in a restaurant league, but he had to give it up when his ankles began to bother him.

Golf became Bobby's favorite sport. He has kidded that if he didn't have a career in food, he would have tried to become a professional golfer. His love for the game dates back to his teenage years when he accompanied his father on outings to the Hamptons—an area of Long Island that includes the towns of Southhampton and East Hampton. His travels have enabled him to play on courses all around the world. But he says that he considers his home course to be the Noyac Golf Club on Long Island.

MARATHON MAN

The high school long distance runner has also continued to run. He participated in the New York City Marathon in 2002, 2006, and 2010. Unfortunately, his inexperience in the event and lack of training hurt him in his first two appearances. He told *Runner's World*, "I remember in 2002 I hit the halfway mark ahead of schedule, thinking that if I walked home from here I'd still be doing okay. But then I just absolutely got crushed." Bobby fared better in 2010. He finished the race with a time of 4:01:37, just shy of his goal of breaking four hours.

Bobby appreciates the health benefits of running. "I'm up at 6 A.M.," he told *Runner's World*, "and I put on my running clothes before I can think about it too much—and just go. I don't schedule any shooting for *Throwdown!* or my other shows until I work out in the morning . . . It keeps me fit for the shows"

THE CHEF AT HOME

In between work and exercise, Flay still finds time to cook for his wife and daughter at home. His involvement with food does not end when his day at the restaurant or television studio is through. He says that cooking for family and friends on Sundays is a real pleasure. In an interview, he explained:

> I love staying at home all Sunday and starting something that takes a long time to cook. You know, from like ten o'clock in the morning. . . . I can put on a game or something and I can hang out with Stephanie. We can read the paper, smell the food as it's sort of coming to fruition. . . . I love those long Sundays that you know at the end of the day it's gonna be about food and some drink.

Both Stephanie and Bobby have favorite foods. She is partial to barbeque and fried chicken. His favorite indulgence is ice cream. "I love to eat it, but I shouldn't," he told *Zalea* magazine. "I don't eat a lot of junk food or fast food, so ice cream is my guilty pleasure."

In helping raise his daughter, Sophie, Bobby has made sure that she learns as much as possible about food. He asserts that it is important for all parents to educate children about eating. The greater the variety of foods that children are exposed to, he says, the more things they'll eat. In 2001

Bobby poses with celebrity chefs Lorena Garcia, Steve Ellis, and Curtis Stone at an event to promote their NBC reality show America's Next Great Restaurant *in 2010. The four chefs were not only judges on the show, but also invested in the winning restaurant idea.* America's Next Great Restaurant *turned out to be something of a disappointment for Bobby; the show's 10 episodes drew poor ratings, and the winning concept, a three-restaurant chain called Soul Daddy, was closed after just a few months in 2011.*

Bobby noted that when his daughter was four years old, she was not a picky eater because he and Sophie's mother exposed her to a variety of foods. "Don't assume kids won't like a food," he advised parents in an Associated Press article. "Sophie loves salty things like capers and olives, which aren't typical 'kid' foods. We found out by trial and error. If you don't do that, the parents are limiting themselves."

Having a famous chef for a father has meant that Sophie has been involved with food her entire life. And Flay has tried to impart his knowledge and expertise in the culinary field to his daughter. However, as of 2011 Sophie has no plans to follow in her father's footsteps. That year Bobby told the *National Ledger*, "Her clear vision is she wants to be a fashion editor at some point. . . . People have always asked her whether she wants to be a chef like her dad, and she always says, 'We already have that covered in our family.'"

On occasion, however, Sophie has played a role in Bobby's projects. In early 2011 she appeared on *America's Next Great Restaurant*. In week seven of the series, the competitors had to create a meal that would appeal to kids. Fourteen-year-old Sophie was on the show as one of the tasters and as a reviewer of restaurant-themed toys.

ADVICE TO ASPIRING CHEFS AND RESTAURATEURS

Flay remains appreciative of what he has achieved and tries to give back to his profession. One way has been by giving advice to young people looking to enter the food profession. Flay usually advises those interested in a culinary career to choose a restaurant that they like and then beg for any possible job in the kitchen, even one that pays nothing. After working in a cooking environment for a while, if they decide that they would still like a career as a chef, they should make the investment to enroll in a culinary school such as the French Culinary Institute.

In November 2010 he told a group of culinary students to be prepared to work long, hard hours with little pay. They also should focus on learning as much as they can: "You are reading cooking magazines and cookbooks on your time off. It becomes your life, so if you are not passionate about it, it's the wrong place to be."

Bobby looks for that passion for cooking when hiring chefs to work in his own restaurants. He says his goal is to develop a pleasant environment in the kitchen where he and his employees can have fun while cooking. So he hires only people who are both ambitious and good-natured. Everything else, including a formal culinary background, is a bonus. He explained in an interview:

> I've hired customers out of the dining room. . . . They'll say, 'I'm an accountant, I hate my job. I've made some money over the years and I'd really like to come and work in the kitchen.' I'll say they can hang out for a few weeks and they'll stay for three years. It's happened to me three or four times.

But Flay advises those with dreams of opening a restaurant of their own to be realistic. "Have twice as much capital as you think you need," he told a *Wall Street Journal* interviewer. He added:

> If you think it's going to take eight months to build the restaurant, know that it's twice that. Expect the unexpected. It will ultimately happen, whether it's the health department [coming in], or the chef quits, or the gas line doesn't work. And go slow. Don't try to feed 300 people the first night. You want to be a good restaurant for 20 years, not 20 weeks.

THINGS TO COME

Although food has been a big part of Bobby's life, he has other ambitions. He has strong feelings about the city where he was born and raised, and is a self-proclaimed news "junkie." These interests may lead him down a new path, such as politics.

"I have a couple of goals," Bobby has said when asked about his future. "With television, I love news and current events. I would love to be in news in some way and talk about things that are not just food. I'm a proud native New Yorker. After my restaurant career I would like to go into politics at some point to help the city."

In the meantime, Bobby is giving back to the community in other ways. He has long supported charities such as Meals-on-Wheels and Citymeals-on-Wheels, which help feed the hungry. In 2003 he decided to do something more. He established the Bobby Flay Scholarship to the French Culinary Institute. The recipient would be a New York City high school student interested in a career in the culinary arts.

Flay has remained appreciative of what the French Culinary Institute did for him and of Joe Allen's generosity in paying his full tuition to the school. In addition to establishing the annual scholarship, he is also personally involved in the selection of the winner. He explained in a *Chef's Story* interview, "I had the idea . . . let's find a student [who] was maybe not necessarily the same position I'm in, but who really wants to go from high school to culinary school . . . and may not be the greatest student from a liberal arts standpoint. And it was really important to me that I pick the student."

Bobby and his wife Stephanie have been active supporters of many charitable causes.

The search for the first scholarship recipient was documented by the Food Network in a special program, *Bobby Flay: Chef Mentor*. In 2005 it won a James Beard Foundation award for a National Television Food Show.

The film showed how the school's CEO, Dorothy Cann Hamilton, helped Bobby select Long Island City High School, where he spent many afternoons teaching lessons and sharing his knowledge with the students in the Careers through Culinary Arts Program (C-Cap). As the end of the school year approached, Bobby told the 16 seniors in the class that he was going to offer a full-tuition scholarship to the French Culinary Institute.

The five students who indicated interest in the scholarship were given a taste of restaurant life by working a lunch shift at Mesa Grill. Bobby would later say that each of them impressed him with their attitude toward the work. Although just one student was chosen for the Flay Scholarship, the other four students also came out winners. With the help of Hamilton and the French Culinary Institute, four more scholarships were found for the others.

CULINARY LEGACY

The Chinese philosopher Confucius said, "Choose a job you love, and you will never have to work a day in your life." Bobby has been fortunate to be one of the lucky ones to have done this. He entered the culinary field purely by chance and made the most of his opportunities. Through hard work and determination, he became financially successful.

But success for Bobby, he has said, would be leaving a signature culinary legacy. If his television audience, cookbook readers, and customers at his restaurants are any judge, he has done just that. "For me, cooking has been everything," he says. "It really has given me a sense of belonging. Among my peers I would like to be known as somebody who is true to my profession, somebody who is a hard worker and who is known for a certain style of cuisine. That would be plenty for me."

CHAPTER NOTES

p. 7: "[T]he phenomenon of the celebrity . . ." Lisa Abend, "The Cult of the Celebrity Chef Goes Global," *Time* (June 21, 2010). http://www.time.com/time/magazine/article/0,9171,1995844,00.html

p. 8: "It's great to be known . . ." Kaoru Hoketsu, *Iron Chef: The Official Book* (New York: Berkeley Publishing Group, 2001), p. xvii.

p. 12: "I cut my finger . . ." "Biography: Bobby Flay Discusses Battling Morimoto," Biography Channel, (1:23 of video). http://www.youtube.com/watch?v=ty2xlbCGIFQ

p. 13: "He's not a chef . . ." "Iron Chef—New York Battle (The Match) (4 of 5)," (4:23 of video). http://www.youtube.com/watch?v=FKkCxjkWX3U

p. 14: ""It was the best . . ." "Biography: Bobby Flay Discusses Battling Morimoto," Biography Channel, (2:47 of video), http://www.youtube.com/watch?v=ty2xlbCGIFQ

p. 17: "I just thought it . . ." Biography: Bobby Flay, A&E Television Networks, (4:13 of video). http://www.biography.com/people/bobby-flay-578278/videos/bobby-flay-full-episode-2072034711

p. 17: "It was at the . . ." Samantha Miller, "Hot Hands: Chef Bobby Flay Sizzles His Way to Culinary Stardom with Spice Southwestern Fare," *People*, July 13, 1998. http://www.people.com/people/archive/article/0,,20125770,00.html

p. 17: "My mom was an . . ." Matt Lee and Ted Lee, "The Chef: Bobby Flay: An Old Favorite Dances to a Southwestern Beat," *New York Times* (January 29, 2003). http://www.nytimes.com/2003/01/29/dining/the-chef-bobby-flay-an-old-favorite-dances-to-a-southwestern-beat.html?pagewanted=print&src=pm

p. 18: "I delivered pizzas . . ." Danyelle Freeman, "Bobby Flay Will be Grillin' and Chillin' at Chelsea Food Fest," *New York Daily News* (October 10, 2008). http://articles.nydailynews.com/2008-10-10/entertainment/17907603_1_south-beach-wine-food-festival-flay

p. 19: "A professional athlete . . ." Freeman, "Bobby Flay Will be Grillin' and Chillin' at Chelsea Food Fest."

p. 19: "We used to have . . ." Sarah Rosenberg and Christina Caron, "Nightline Platelist: Bobby Flay," ABC News Nightline (June 9, 2008). http://abcnews.go.com/Nightline/OnTheRoad/nightline-platelist-bobby-flay/story?id=5031981

p. 19: "People [who] don't know . . ." "Here's Bobby," Chefography: Bobby Flay, (0:29 of video). http://www.foodnetwork.com/videos/heres-bobby/36226.html

p. 21: "My sense was Joe . . ." Biography: Bobby Flay, A&E Television

Networks, (5:24 of video).

p. 21:   "The busboy had to . . ." Bobby Flay, "Finding Keys to Success," Guideposts, http://www.guideposts.org/celebrities/motivational-story-about-bobby-flay-finding-success-after-dropping-out-school

p. 22:   "I remember waking up . . ." Flay, "Finding Keys to Success."

p. 26:   "I convinced my father . . ." Michael Procopio, "A Conversation with Dorothy Cann Hamilton," *Bay Area Bites* (May 25, 2007). http://blogs.kqed.org/bayareabites/2007/05/25/a-conversation-with-dorothy-cann-hamilton/

p. 27:   "was ridiculous, because . . ." Biography: Bobby Flay, A&E Television Networks, (11:33 of video).

p. 28:   "He's fired . . ." Flay, "Finding Keys to Success."

p. 28:   "I was 20 years . . ." Colleen DeBaise, "How a Famous Foodie Got His Start," *The Wall Street Journal* (April 2011). http://online.wsj.com/article/SB10001424052748704570704576274822558736018.html

p. 29:   "California cuisine is . . ." David Zuckerman, "New York Restaurants Ride California Wave: Trendsetters Luring West's Chefs," *Nation's Restaurant News* (January 6, 1986). http://findarticles.com/p/articles/mi_m3190/is_v20/ai_4091094/

p. 29:   "Whoever said chefs of the . . ." Alex Witchel, "How a Celebrity Chef of the 80's Got His Stove Back," *New York Times* (April 17, 2002). http://www.nytimes.com/2002/04/17/dining/how-a-celebrity-chef-of-the-80-s-got-his-stove-back.html

p. 30:   "I loved the camaraderie . . ." Andrea Weigl, "An Interview with Celebrity Chef Bobby Flay," *Catholic Online*, (October 28, 2008). http://www.catholic.org/hf/home/story.php?id=30269

p. 31:   "They introduced me . . ." Bobby Flay and Joan Schwartz, *Bobby Flay's Bold American Food: More than 200 Revolutionary Recipes* (New York: Grand Central Publishing, 1994), p. ix.

p. 31:   "It was closed on Sundays . . ." Flay, "Finding Keys to Success."

p. 32:   "I was a New York . . ." Lee and Lee, "The Chef: Bobby Flay: An Old Favorite Dances to a Southwestern Beat."

p. 34:   "I remember having . . ." Gina DiNunno, "Next Food Network Star's Bobby Flay: Being in Front of the Camera Is 'Very Hard,'" *TV Guide* (June 3, 2010). http://www.tvguide.com/News/Bobby-Flay-Food-Star-1019208.aspx

p. 35:   "I have a great deal . . ." Trish Hall, "Sharing a Life of Chefs' Hours and Pancakes," *New York Times* (May 8, 1991). http://www.nytimes.com/1991/05/08/garden/sharing-a-life-of-chefs-hours-and-pancakes.html

p. 37:   "I imagined soaring ceilings . . ." Bobby Flay, *Bobby Flay's Mesa Grill Cookbook* (New York, Clarkson Potter/Publishers, 2007), p. 1.

p. 38:   "Do it with him . . ." Flay, "Finding Keys to Success."

p. 39:   "Jerry said, 'Let's wake this . . ." Biography: Bobby Flay, A&E Television Networks, (21:33 of video).

p. 39: "Although New York was in . . ." Flay, *Bobby Flay's Mesa Grill Cookbook*, p. 3.

p. 39: "the sassy Tex-Mex fare . . ." "Bobby Flay," *New York Times*, http://topics.nytimes.com/top/reference/timestopics/people/f/bobby_flay/index.html

p. 40: "The roasted corn fresh from . . ." Flay, *Bobby Flay's Mesa Grill Cookbook*, p. 3.

p. 40: "My first take on Bobby . . ." Samantha Miller, "Hot Hands," *People* (July 13, 1998). http://www.people.com/people/archive/article/0,,20125770,00.html

p. 41: "We looked at 50 . . ." Peter O. Keegan, "Ole! Flay, Kretchmer Bring Spanish Flair to Bolo," *Nation's Restaurant News* (December 6, 1993). http://findarticles.com/p/articles/mi_m3190/is_n48_v27/ai_14692113/

p. 43: "Spain is the forgotten culinary . . ." Keegan, "Ole! Flay, Kretchmer Bring Spanish Flair to Bolo."

p. 44: "To celebrate, nurture, and preserve . . ." Mission Statement of the James Beard Foundation, http://www.jamesbeard.org/index.php?q=aboutus

p. 44: "The new tapas menu shows . . ." William Grimes, "New Tapas Menu Sets Off the Fireworks," *New York Times* (June 4, 2003). http://www.nytimes.com/2003/06/04/dining/restaurants-new-tapas-menu-sets-off-the-fireworks.html

p. 45: "All my friends told me . . ." "Late Night Eats: Bobby Flay Answers Your Twitter Questions," *Late Night with Jimmy Fallon* (November 30, 2010), 1:14 of video, http://eater.com/archives/2010/11/30/bobby-flay-fifteen-year-old-paella-disaster.php

p. 48: "It's a complicated situation . . ." Lois Smith Brady, "Vows: Kate Connelly and Bobby Flay," *New York Times* (October 15, 1995). http://www.nytimes.com/1995/10/15/style/vows-kate-connelly-and-bobby-flay.html

p. 50: "The Food Network opened in . . ." Chef's Story: Bobby Flay, Soho Culinary Productions (32:50 of video).

p. 51: "by traveling around the country . . ." Bobby Flay, *Bobby Flay's Throwdown!* (New York, Clarkson Potter/Publishers, 2010), p. 9.

p. 52: "The one thing I decided . . ." David Bianculli, "Thriller from The Grillers Iron Chef & Flay Cross Spatulas," *New York Daily News* (May 30, 2001). http://articles.nydailynews.com/2001-05-30/entertainment/18167350_1_kitchen-stadium-flay-japanese-cooking-show

p. 54: "I'm from New York . . ." Chef's Story: Bobby Flay, Soho Culinary Productions (36:28 of video).

p. 56: "grilling is not really the . . ." Jocelyn Morse, "Bobby Flay Interview," StarChefs.com. http://www.starchefs.com/chefs/BFlay/html/interview.shtml

p. 56: "the most famous grill-meister . . ." Chef's Story: Bobby Flay, Soho

Culinary Productions (0:01 of video).

p. 57:   "I tried to grill scrambled . . ." Stephanie Sayfie Aagaard, "Bobby
         Flay Talks Food," *Ocean Drive Magazine*.
         http://www.oceandrive.com/celebrities/articles/bobby-flay

p. 60:   "Bobby Flay's new Mesa Grill . . ." "Bobby Flay to Open First
         Restaurant Outside of New York at Caesars Palace; Acclaimed Mesa
         Grill to Debut in Spring 2004," *Business Wire* (July 10, 2003).
         http://www.businesswire.com/news/home/20030710005260/en/Bobby
         -Flay-Open-Restaurant-York-Caesars-Palace

p. 66:   "In Paris this meant that . . ." Stephanie Remige, "Interview with
         Neil Manacle," Shiftdrink.com. http://www.stephanieremige.com/
         Stephanie_Remige/Restaurant_Clips.html

p. 67:   "Every restaurant gets four . . ." Chef's Story: Bobby Flay, Soho
         Culinary Productions (7:02 of video).

p. 68:   "Stephanie, Miriam and I sort . . ." Richard Leong, "World Chefs:
         Flay Learns from Losing to Other Chefs," Reuters (October 26,
         2010). http://www.reuters.com/article/2010/10/26/us-chefs-flay-
         idUSTRE69P2MQ20101026

p. 68:   "*Throwdown!* really is not . . ." Leong, "World Chefs: Flay Learns
         from Losing to Other Chefs."

p. 69:   "They need to be able . . ." Tiffany N. D'Emidio, "Interview: Bobby
         Flay Talks Next Food Network Star," *Eclipse Magazine* (June 22,
         2009). http://eclipsemagazine.com/hollywood-insider/10885/

p. 72:   "First and foremost I . . ."Charles Thorp, "Interview with Chef
         Bobby Flay About Bobby Flay Steak, the 5th Burger Palace and the
         Obamas," Examiner.com (December 2, 2009).
         http://www.examiner.com/ny-in-new-york/interview-with-chef-bobby-
         flay-about-bobby-flay-steak-the-5th-burger-palace-and-the-obamas

p. 75:   "It defies common sense . . ." Stephanie Sayfie Aagaard, "Bobby Flay
         Talks Food," *Ocean Drive Magazine*,
         http://www.oceandrive.com/celebrities/articles/bobby-flay

p. 76:   "His natural style, humor and . . ." "Renowned Chef Bobby Flay to
         Host Exclusive Five-Week Series of Shows on SIRIUS XM Radio,"
         PR Newswire (January 6, 2009). http://investor.sirius.com/releasede-
         tail.cfm?releaseid=357746

p. 78:   "Cooking at the White House . . ." Rene Lynch, "A Presidential 'Iron
         Chef America'," *Los Angeles Times* (January 1, 2010).
         http://articles.latimes.com/2010/jan/01/entertainment/la et iron
         chef1-2010jan01

p. 83:   "I think that's part . . ." Erin Biglow, "America's Next Great
         Restaurant: Interview with Bobby Flay and Steve Ells," *Poptimal*
         (March 1, 2011). http://poptimal.com/2011/03/americas-next-great-
         restaurant-interview-with-bobby-flay-and-steve-ells/

p. 86:   "People need a label . . ." Nancy Weingartner, "Talking with Bobby
         Flay," *Franchise Times* (January 2007).
         http://www.franchisetimes.com/content/story.php?article=00152

p. 86: "When I opened Mesa Grill . . ." Chef's Story: Bobby Flay, Soho Culinary Productions (3:22 of "Questions and Answers" section of video).

p. 86: "shoot a little . . ." Weingartner, "Talking with Bobby Flay."

p. 87: "She said to me . . ." Jo Piazza, "Bobby's Palace," Hamptons Magazine, http://www.hamptons-magazine.com/features/articles/bobbys-palace

p. 88: "Inside it's like a little . . ." Piazza, "Bobby's Palace"

p. 90: "I remember in 2002 . . ." Yishane Lee, "I'm a Runner: Bobby Flay," *Runner's World* (November 2010). http://www.runnersworld.com/article/0,7120,s6-243-544--13690-0,00.html

p. 91: "I'm up at 6 A.M. . . ." Lee, "I'm a Runner: Bobby Flay."

p. 91: "I love staying at home . . ." Chef's Story: Bobby Flay, Soho Culinary Productions (45:00 of video).

p. 91: "I love to eat it . . ." Stuart Reb Donald, "Flay Does It His Way: Interview with Chef Bobby Flay," *Zalea* (October 2007). http://wannabetvchef.com/?p=182

p. 92: "Don't assume kids won't . . ." Associated Press, "The Kitchen: Where Kids Learn of Living," *Los Angeles Times* (January 1, 2001). http://articles.latimes.com/2001/jan/13/home/hm-11691

p. 93: "Her clear vision is . . ." Marilyn Beck and Stacy Jenel Smith, "Bobby Flay Insists Daughter Sophie Was Fair on America's Next Great Restaurant," *National Ledger* (April 23, 2011). http://www.nationalledger.com/pop-culture-news/bobby-flay-insists-daughter-so-118025.shtml

p. 93: "You are reading cooking . . ." Andrea Weigl, "Flay's Passion Still Cookin'" *News Observer*, November 10, 2010, http://www.newsobserver.com/2010/11/10/792130/flays-passion-still-cookin.html

p. 94: "I've hired customers out of . . ." Morse, "Bobby Flay Interview"

p. 94: "Have twice as much . . ." Colleen DeBaise, "How a Famous Foodie Got His Start," *The Wall Street Journal* (April 21, 2011). http://online.wsj.com/article/SB10001424052748704570704576274822558736018.html

p. 95: "I have a couple of . . ." Richard Leong, "Flay Looks Back Through Mellowed Lens," Reuters (October 16, 2007). http://www.reuters.com/article/2007/10/16/us-food-chefs-flay-idUSN1533070220071016

p. 95: "I had the idea . . ." Chef's Story: Bobby Flay, Soho Culinary Productions (50:12 of video).

p. 97: "Choose a job you love . . ." "Confucius: Quotes," Goodreads.com, http://www.goodreads.com/author/quotes/15321.Confucius

p. 97: "For me, cooking . . ." Dorothy Hamilton, Patric Kuh, Matthew Septimus, *27 Chefs Talk About What Got Them into the Kitchen* (New York: Soho Culinary Productions, 2007), p. 133.

CHRONOLOGY

1964: Robert William Flay is born in New York City on December 10.

1982: Flay gets his first professional restaurant job at Joe Allen Restaurant.

1984: In August Flay graduates from the French Culinary Institute in New York City.

1991: The Mesa Grill opens in New York on January 15.

1993: The Bolo Restaurant and Bar opens in November; Flay is named the James Beard Foundation's Rising Star Chef of the Year.

1994: Flay's first cookbook, *Bobby Flay's Bold American Food*, is published in May.

1996: Flay's daughter, Sophie, is born on April 16; Flay cohosts his first Food Network show, *Grillin' & Chillin'*, with Jack McDavid.

2000: The controversial Iron Chef special "New York Battle" is broadcast.

2005: Flay marries Stephanie March on February 20; in April he opens Bar Americain in New York City; in May he wins an Emmy for Outstanding Service Show Host for *Boy Meets Grill*.

2006: *Throwdown! with Bobby Flay* debuts on the Food Network; Bobby Flay Steak opens in Atlantic City, New Jersey, in July.

2008: The first Bobby's Burger Palace opens in Lake Grove, New York, on July 15.

2010: *Brunch @ Bobby's* debuts on the Cooking Channel.

2011: Flay hosts *America's Next Great Restaurant*, which airs on NBC from March until May.

BOXTY PANCAKE—a traditional Irish potato pancake.

BRASSERIE—an informal French restaurant with a large selection of drinks.

BÛCHE DE NOËL—the French name for a traditional Christmas cake, made with a chocolate butter-cream and decorated to look like a Yule log.

CHEF DE PARTIE—a chef in charge of a particular station or area of production in a kitchen.

CHICKEN TIKKA MASALA—a curry dish in which roasted chicken chunks are served in a creamy, tomato-based sauce.

CUISINE—a style of cooking characteristic of a particular country or region.

DINGLE PIE—a small Irish meat pie usually made with lamb.

GOURMET—a person devoted to the consumption of fine food and drink.

HORS D'OEUVRE—a small savory dish, usually served as an appetizer before a meal.

MARINADE—a liquid, usually containing vinegar and oil with various spices and herbs, in which a food is soaked before it is cooked.

MEISTER—a person skilled in a specified area of activity.

MERINGUE—a topping for pies made of beaten egg whites and sugar, and usually baked until brown.

GLOSSARY

PAELLA—a saffron-flavored Spanish dish made with meat, seafood, vegetables and rice.

QUESADILLA—a tortilla filled with a combination of cheese and/or beans.

SAVORY—salty or spicy, but not sweet.

SOUS CHEF—a chef in a restaurant who is second in authority below the head chef.

SURF AND TURF—a dish containing steak and seafood, usually lobster.

TAPAS—small, savory Spanish dishes, usually served with drinks at a bar.

DeWitt, Dave. *The Southwest Table: Traditional Cuisine from Texas, New Mexico, and Arizona*. Guilford, Conn.: Lyons Press, 2011.

Flay, Bobby. *Bobby Flay's Mesa Grill Cookbook*. New York: Clarkson Potter/Publishers, 2007.

Flay, Bobby, Stephanie Banyas, and Miriam Garron. *Bobby Flay's Throwdown!* New York: Clarkson Potter/Publishers, 2010.

Hoketsu, Kaoru. *Iron Chef: The Official Book*. New York: Berkeley Publishing Group, 2001.

Morimoto, Masaharu. *Morimoto: The New Art of Japanese Cooking*. New York: DK Publishing, 2007.

Ruhlman, Michael. *The Reach of a Chef*. New York: Penguin, 2007.

Waxman, Jonathan. *A Great American Cook: Recipes from the Home Kitchen of One of Our Most Influential Chefs*. Foreword by Bobby Flay. New York: Houghton Mifflin, 2007.

INTERNET RESOURCES

HTTP://WWW.BOBBYFLAY.COM/

The official website of chef Bobby Flay includes information about his restaurants, television shows, and recipes.

HTTP://WWW.COOKINGCHANNELTV.COM/

The official website of the Cooking Channel contains information about network shows, chefs, and recipes.

HTTP://WWW.FOODNETWORK.COM/

The official website of the Food Network contains information about network shows, chefs, and recipes.

HTTP://WWW.FRENCHCULINARY.COM/

The official website of the French Culinary Institute includes information about the faculty and staff, courses of study, and admission procedures.

HTTP://JOEALLENRESTAURANT.COM

The official website of Joe Allen Restaurant, where Bobby Flay got his start.

Numbers in **bold italics** refer to captions.

JOHN F. GRABOWSKI is a native of Brooklyn, New York. He holds a bachelor's degree in psychology from City College of New York and a master's degree in educational psychology from Teachers College, Columbia University. He was a teacher for 39 years, as well as a freelance writer, specializing in the fields of sports, education, and comedy.

Grabowski's published work includes 55 books; a nationally syndicated sports column; consultation on several math textbooks; articles for newspapers, magazines, and the programs of professional sports teams; and comedy material sold to Jay Leno, Joan Rivers, Yakov Smirnoff, and numerous other comics. He and his wife, Patricia, live in Staten Island with their daughter, Elizabeth.